GLUE

The stuff that binds us together
to do extraordinary work

Tracey Ezard

2017

Copyright 2017 Tracey Ezard

www.traceyezard.com
First published in 2017

All rights reserved. No part of this publication may be reproduced, stored in a retrieval system or transmitted in any form by any means, electronic, mechanical, photocopy, recording or otherwise, without the prior written permission of the copyright owner, except as provided by international copyright law.

Author:	Tracey Ezard
Title:	Glue: the stuff that binds us together to do extraordinary work
ISBN:	978-0-6487931-1-3
Subjects:	Organisation
	Leadership
	Collaboration
	Learning
	Workplace relations
	Teamwork
	Conversations
Cover design:	Matt Emery
Illustrations:	Tracey Ezard
Reviewer:	Kath Walters
Typesetting:	Lu Sexton

For Justin, Conor and Layla
I am because of who we are

Contents

Introduction — vii

PART I – WHY WE NEED GLUE

1. We don't need conventional teams; we need 21st-Century tribes — 13
2. Silos create stagnation — 37
3. From territorial to transformational leadership — 57

PART II – THE GLUE OF COLLABORATION

4. Culture and strategy should eat breakfast together — 79
5. The dangerous illusion of collaboration — 101
6. Collaborative inquiry and deeper learning — 131

PART III – THE GLUE OF TRUST

A little segue before launching into part three — 157
7. Connection — 163
8. Compassion — 183
9. Conversation — 205

Conclusion — 231

Introduction

I have written this book for leaders and teams who want to create something extraordinary with each other, but are not sure how. What they do know is that relationships are important. They understand that the environment we create in our workplaces is linked to wellbeing and working in more intelligent ways. They are frustrated with silos – the attitude that occurs when departments or groups within an organisation do not want to share information and knowledge with each other. They want to collaborate more but are not exactly sure what that looks like. They also want to make an impact. These people are committed to doing their very best, wherever they sit on the journey to high performance.

This book is for teams who want to lift beyond convention. They want to work differently, let go of the rules and structures that keep them mediocre, and move with momentum. These teams want to find the glue that will help them provide a service to their clients that is more than excellent.

In a fast-moving world, collaboration is key. We need savvy, smart thinking and ways of working that blur lines between people, tasks and departments now more than ever. Disruptors are upsetting the previous even keel of every sector. The ability to be flexible and open, to learn new ways of working and to create a buzz around the work is critical to thriving in this chaotic environment.

Fear drives many organisations. Fear of raising issues, rocking the boat and moving out of default comfortable behaviour. There are thousands of teams who have no autonomy over their work, are treated like children and head to work with dread every day. Distrust and disconnection are daily issues that create stress and a lack of commitment to our jobs. It's time for us to change this paradigm. Humans crave connection. We crave relationships that support us and value our unique qualities. We want to belong, and we want to do our best. We just need the nutrients and fertile soil to grow.

My background in education, and specifically in building collaborative staff learning cultures, makes me passionate about creating environments where people thrive – not just survive. I have seen leaders who can bring out the best in their people, and others who prefer to use control and command to force their agenda forward. That military paradigm of leadership no longer serves us. The impact on the engagement and motivation with this approach is detrimental not only to the bottom line but also to health. My many years working with leaders has helped me identify the key elements that are in place when we are pushing the status quo and providing the safety nets that allow people to learn and collaborate deeply. We are in an environment where agility, flexibility and innovation are the winning ingredients.

The first section of this book outlines why creating a strong connection within our organisations is crucial in today's business context. It outlines why we need to think beyond high performance and conventional teams. We need to create 21st-Century Tribes. The second part is devoted to the concepts of culture and strategy and the elements that bring them together with strength – collaboration and learning. The final section delves into the foundational glue of 21st-Century Tribes – the glue of trust.

Tracey Ezard

Working as a leader in the education, automotive and hospitality industries prior to this work gave me a unique perspective of purpose-driven organisations that galvanise around something beyond profit. It opened my eyes to the invisible threads that draw people together to trust each other enough to take risks and step outside their comfort zone.

From a lifetime of facilitation and culture building, I understand the challenges of bringing people together and spurring them towards great outcomes. I help leaders and teams set the frameworks for collaboration and create environments to do amazing things.

I have had the honour of working with thousands of leaders and hundreds of teams over the last decade and seen the power that strong connection to purpose and each other can have. I love working with teams that want to be better. They want to co-create the future together and gain serious momentum in getting there. They want to co-create the culture and the strategy to do extraordinary work.

This book shows where to focus the attention of leaders, teams, and project teams so that they become 21st-Century tribes, able to deal with the complexities of the world with enthusiasm, deep trust and impact. These tribes build the glue of collaboration and trust and challenge each other to evolve and grow constantly.

Part I
Why we need Glue

1

we don't need conventional teams; we need 21st-Century tribes

Moving to warp speed

The need for speed in the world today means every organisation and business must work in a faster and more connected way. All sectors need to work swiftly and adapt to changing contexts. Yet our current hierarchical approach stymies any creative thinking from the people on lower rungs of the ladder. Hefty bureaucratic processes slow things down. Default thinking and ways of working mean we waste time and energy on things that don't matter. Lack of cultural growth and engagement in organisations creates stagnation. Low engagement brings no traction to businesses needing to speed up and stay with the wave of global transformation.

The imperative of being able to work in a more flexible and agile way in the world today is well documented. Ever increasing technology advancement, global disruption to industries and increased consumer choice are causing both chaos and opportunity for organisations in all sectors. Technology democratisation gives everyone the world in their pocket. What's out there is coming to me rather than me having to go out there and find it. Markets are demanding choice, high-quality service and value for money. Customers walk with their market share elsewhere to get what they need and what they want.

Glue

Back in the workplace, we sit through meetings with repetitive agendas, listening to people drone on about tasks that don't value add to what we need to do. Most of us are tempted to face plant onto the table in frustration or boredom. The important work to be done is mentioned fleetingly at the end of the meeting when we've run out of time. We nod to each other that we'll get to that critical discussion next meeting. Back at our desks we hurriedly complete a siloed task before the next meeting of no consequence is due. Decisions take a torturous route on their way to being made, delayed through micromanagement and a tight control fixation. This creates frustration and lag in response to changing contexts and consumer needs.

Sound familiar?

> When teams don't feel connected or engaged with their work or leaders, creativity and innovation fail to ignite.

People are demanding more of workplaces. We want a connection to purpose. We want to connect to what the business is doing and feel like we're contributing. We are also craving for more connection to each other.

New employees come out of the education system familiar and savvy with technology and what technology can achieve. They have also been through an education system focused for the last decade on fostering thinking skills – critical analysis and collaborative problem-solving. Many managers and leaders are not skilled in either keeping up with technology leaps nor the facilitation of collaborative learning environments that bring out the best in people.

21st-Century Tribes

The companies that are setting the standard are creating high-performance teams. They understand a high-performance environment that will sustain future success needs a future focused approach. They need 21st-Century Tribes.

21st-Century Tribes connect quickly to the higher purpose and each other. They concentrate on building strong relationships that bring about the glue of trust. They create an environment where team learning, curiosity and collaboration is in the DNA of how they work. They bring new and transient members into the team in a way that allows for time-limited projects and the 'gig economy' to flourish. They constantly go back to purpose and understanding why they are undertaking courses of action. They invite creativity and innovation. They value the customer and the purpose beyond all else and have outstanding ability to empathise.

If we know this, we can understand where to put our focus when we want momentum in our organisation. Not just shuffling people around, but creating real change in the way we work. Our work becomes about delighting the customer, fulfilling the needs and wants that the customer has, rather than just outputs. In the not for profit, government and human services sectors, it is all about the client – whether it be critical services for our most vulnerable, providing water, roads, health care or education.

Clue

Now is the time to move

HOW we do this work is changing and if we don't shift our most foundational systems and behaviours, we will become, outdated, outwitted and outsmarted – and obsolete.

Companies' relevancy will be reliant on teams being able to move in an agile and flexible way and being able to respond to context. Businesses are moving to a more project- and matrix-oriented way, where they can move people where they need them. They tap into the skills and the value that people bring, rather than proclaiming, 'This is your role, and that's the only role you're going to have'. This 20th-century paradigm decrees, 'It's the role, not the person'. Whereas 21st-Century Tribes look at the skills the person brings, and how we utilise these skills and their attributes in the best way possible. Businesses that can move resources and people where they need to be, tap into the skills and innovations that will win the game.

> A new organizational model is on the rise: a 'network of teams' in which companies build and empower teams to work on specific business projects and challenges. These networks are aligned and coordinated with operations and information centers similar to command centers in the military. Indeed, in some ways, businesses are becoming more like Hollywood movie production teams and less like traditional corporations, with people coming together to tackle projects, then disbanding and moving on to new assignments once the project is complete.
>
> Global Human Capital Trends, 2016. Deloitte

Agile movement

Historically, teams have worked in siloed environments where one team is responsible for one component, and another team in charge of the next. Stories of products being late to market because of a lack of communication along the development chain are rife in industries such as telecommunications and banking. Being able to move people between teams and projects, so we get the conversation happening faster and quicker, and we get the inputs critical along the way, is the game changer for a lot of organisations. Project-based work where people come together around a purpose and then move back to their teams, creates the environment where things must happen in a faster, more connected way. Having outside expertise come in either as a consultant arrangement or as a partnership and collaboration, is another way businesses are organising themselves differently. We're leapfrogging to the next level by responding quickly to higher expectation.

The mindset of the future – now

Culturally, the ability to be able to push the status quo as a team is the mindset of the future. We must challenge our assumptions, challenge the way we work, and create a different way of thinking and doing. Or consumers will make their choice, and they'll move away. Other places will step up and say, 'We can provide that'. When we don't push at the status quo, we start to lose market share, and then we're also playing catch-up. Suddenly we've gone from leader to follower, or from good market to poor market.

The flipside of this is when we create an environment where it's an exciting place to push at the edges of the way we've always worked; it becomes about market-leading rather than market-following.

Glue

We create an environment that people want to be a part of. We attract great people. It compels the best talent to come and work.

> When we get this happening this virtuous cycle builds on itself. We attract people who help us become more and more innovative and agile.

We attract workers who are willing to take risks, and be real learners in the space, rather than having people who are happy with status quo. The orthodox approaches we've always done in the past are not getting the results that we're after anymore.

Reinvention and re-imagination are the point that most organisations are at. Let's not just plateau and go into irrelevance. Let's reinvent and reimagine where we are.

Shift or oblivion beckons

When I was at university in the 80s, I worked in one of Melbourne's first video shops. It was the very beginning of the video industry. People would queue out of the shop, waiting for us to use the infant computer program created to track the rentals. It crashed regularly but was such a novelty people didn't mind waiting! People would get either VHS or Beta tapes depending on the type of machine they had. The Beta users were the true early adopters of the technology. When the store first opened, we stocked as many Beta tapes as VHS. Within two years, we would stock eight VHS and two Beta copies of new releases, much to the annoyance of the Beta owners. They had to move to VHS before long and probably became the people at the front of the line of each Apple product launch. As soon as the new releases were on the shelf, they were grabbed. A long wait list was placed in a diary, as people planned their movies nights around availability. It was an interesting and exciting time. Our stores were like parties. Friday night was a highlight for all of us – customers and staff. It was great working on a Friday night. People would come in groups to find the best movies. The latest releases were up on the screen. In another part of the store, music was pumping. We grew to a chain of about five or six shops quickly in the very early days of the industry.

Customers would have their favourite staff member. They would go back to them the following week, and ask, 'Tell us another one you love'. It was a movement. The video industry grew to a billion-dollar industry globally. Then, of course, the bigger chains started consuming the smaller ones, as happens, and huge organisations, chains from the US came in, such as Blockbuster Video, to gobble up all the competition. It also became much easier to get videos. Even the corner store started renting them. About the mid-00s, the industry ultimately faltered, and people stopped going to the video shop. The industry was at saturation point. Then came video downloads – both legal and illegal. Australia became the illegal download king of the world, adding to the industry's woes. Chains like Blockbuster Video and Video Ezy, part of that multi-billion-dollar industry started to divest, and in the end, declined. Blockbuster Video in Australia went into video kiosks to move with the times and you will still see the kiosks around. But as an industry, it became dead in the water.

Clue

Staying great

Author Jim Collins examined 60 great companies in his two books, *Good to Great* and *Built to Last*. Some of them, unfortunately, were not built to last, such as Fannie Mae's, Federal National Mortgage Association in the USA, which collapsed during the Global Financial Crisis of 2008. In his last book, *How the Mighty Fall*, Collins identifies the five stages in the process of decline in the 11 of 60 companies that did not stay 'great'.

Stage one is the 'Hubris of Success' – companies firmly believing in their superiority and that the way they do business is the best way – they fail to test their 'assumptions' and stay in learning mode.

Stage two is about greediness – the 'Undisciplined Pursuit of More'. Moving into other industries where the success formula doesn't apply or expanding without maintaining excellence. Confusing big with great.

Stage three is the 'Denial of Risk and Peril'. Classic ostrich behaviour which sees data pointing to a decline blamed on external factors or ignored completely. Large risks are undertaken without rigorous testing. Shifting contexts are ignored.

Stage four 'Grasping for Salvation' is the stage of panic and silver bullet chasing. Leadership changes herald saviour leaders, and there is a general gnashing of teeth to jump on a saving strategy.

Stage five is the grim 'Capitulation to Irrelevance or Death'. Say no more – the majority of the video industry reached this stage in the 2000s.

Tracey Ezard

The disruption effect

Several disruptors spring to mind that are sending shudders through other industries. Uber and AirBnB have both the taxi and hotel industry respectively suffering from at least stage one and two, with stage three and four behaviours popping up around the world. Blockchain, a peer to peer network for transferring ownership of goods and confirming financial transactions is currently disrupting supply chain processes, not by disrupting business models, but providing a completely new foundational economic system.

For the video industry, it was first mail-order DVD rental services, started by an annoyed Blockbuster customer Reed Hastings. He had received a $40 overdue fee. His company, Netflix, went on to dominate the online streaming that finally signalled the major players in the video store industry's 'Capitulation to Irrelevance and Death'. The video stores that are surviving and even creating a cult following are those who have carved a niche for themselves in their local area. On a side note, they are also continuing to provide something that is disrupting those who are moving to a fully digital presence – the human connection.

For the video industry, the 1980s and 1990s were a great time. It was a huge, profitable curve up. The industry was incredibly innovative. Excellent computer programming went with it, as well as distribution agreements with the major companies such as Warner Bros. Great customer service and easy access to the latest movies got huge market share. Innovation was no longer a focus, and it started to coast. Instead of looking at what was going on around with a real eagle eye, and keeping the innovation as a top priority, it fell into status quo thinking and classic stage one and two behaviours. The large players expanded into huge companies

Glue

that were too large to shift. The majority failed to keep an eye on the market and technology, and say, 'How do we change the business model so that we can continue?'

Ways to fade into mediocrity and oblivion

Success now is not an indicator of success in the future. That's something we need to watch. Innovation in the past is great, but continuing to always look at how do we do things differently, and continuous improvement and ongoing change is the measure.

Here are some sure-fire ways to become a Blockbuster:

Stick with the status quo

Beware the arrogance of success. 'Our strategy is sound; we are the experts in our field. We give everyone what they need.' A patronising approach to saying we'll tell you what you need, rather than listening. That closes down growth, doesn't foster innovation mindset, or a customer-centric mindset.

Beware the comfort of Status Quo. The assumption (or hope!) that change is a one-off, rather than an organisational principle keeps us stuck in status quo.

Change structure but not behaviours

Conventional wisdom says that if things aren't working, restructure! We've got engagement surveys that say, 'Our people aren't engaged, our consumers aren't happy, we must change structures'. Executives get out the organisational chart and do a bit of a reshuffle. They change teams, and they change leaders, but the same problems still occur. People remain disconnected from each other. People are still working with their heads down rather than their heads up, and they're isolated. The Deloitte Report on Global Human Capital Trends 2016, covering over 7,000 business and HR leaders, cites 77% of organisations have recently or are in the middle of a restructure, but only 19% of them think they have the right culture. As companies strive to become more agile and customer-focused, organisations are shifting their structures from traditional, functional models toward interconnected, flexible teams. More than nine out of ten executives surveyed (92%) rate organisational design as a top priority, and nearly half (45%) report their companies are either in the middle of a restructuring (39%) or planning one (6%).

There seems to be something very wrong with that. People are just shuffling deck chairs and they're not changing mindset. They're not changing the way that they work. To do this, we need to be okay not to have the answers. Be okay with a bit of confusion and sit with not knowing. Be prepared to tweak things, putting in clear feedback loops to evaluate if you have the impact you are after. Then, work together to find ways to move forward. Rather than having everything set in stone, go with a little bit of 'try it and see' in the mix.

Silo innovation

In 21st-Century Tribe environments, innovation is everywhere. A lot of organisations have innovation in just another silo. Disconnected from the real work and the people doing the real work. The innovation silo. When we create every team into a learning team, innovation is learning. Innovation is simply doing things in a different way, and learning from what you know, and thinking of different ways to do it. You need to have a learning mindset to do that, and a collaborative mindset to do that. When we tap into what other people think as well, we expand the way that we work.

Clue

Keep an illusion of competence

Default thinking prevents us from using the same systems that don't work. We suffer from the illusion of competence – which says we have all the answers ourselves and get it right all the time. We need to build the ability to collaborate with each other to solve problems. It's like we're stuck in a rut. 'I must sort it out myself.' Unless it is a mindful ritual, we don't talk explicitly with each other about how we can all work together to get a good outcome.

Leaders also give the impression that if everyone else changes we will all be fine. Restructures are reactions unless there is a focus on restructuring mindsets, beliefs and behaviours. Laughingly called the 'soft skills', they are the hardest things to change. And to change leadership behaviours first is critical to change culture.

> If leaders don't feel the need to change themselves, they won't get change in the organisation.

Most people are not skilled at having the self-awareness that the first thing you need to change is the way you work.

We are right slap bang in the middle of new circumstances, new paradigms. Comfort-zone thinking will help us fall into decline and entropy. We need to shake up our thinking and look beyond the comfortable.

The comfort of 'no' and the safety of bureaucracy

Simon is head of food services at a large health network. They had been playing around with PDSA, which is an improvement cycle: Plan-Do-Study-Act. It looks at how we can implement small innovations that can make a significant impact. Simon and his food services team have been doing a lot of these 'tweaks' with great success, but unfortunately further up the bureaucracy tree hadn't bought into it. Systemic bureaucracy was getting in the way yet again!

One of the main feedback complaints Simon and his team received was about the temperature of the coffee and tea. If you've ever experienced hospital food, you'll know lukewarm is pretty much the benchmark.

The cups were filled in the kitchens, and by the time they got up to the wards, the temperature had reached a lovely tepid temperature. That was something the food services team wanted to change. They put urns into the wards. The food services staff would come up from kitchens, and do the cups of tea and coffee on the wards. In one ward the urn was too small for the number of people on the ward. They tried to get a bigger one, but procurement required higher authority than the Nurse Unit Manager to sign off over $1000. It was escalated up to the site manager. The site manager just didn't want to know about it, said, 'No, not interested'.

Dr Jason Fox, in his brilliant book *How to Lead a Quest: A handbook for pioneering executives* attributes this default thinking of 'computer says no' to apathy and the non-participation in meaningful progress. His premise is that 'our default is the option that we choose automatically in the absence of viable alternatives'.

Clue

And so, Simon, being the pioneering executive that Dr Fox encourages us to be, looked to making his solution a 'viable alternative option' that the more senior leader would buy into. He popped his head into the Director of Site Operations, and said, 'Can we catch up for a meeting, and can I bring you a cup of coffee?' She said, 'Sure, that would be great'. He bought her a cup of coffee from the kitchen that had spent the same amount of time getting to her as it did to the patients. The fearless leader took a sip and made a comment about the temperature of it. Simon made it clear that this was what the patients were receiving. He outlined the current situation and the form was signed immediately. Simon, of course, had one on him!

Simon was thinking out of the box, thinking differently about how he could get around bureaucracy and default NO thinking. He also demonstrated another of Dr Fox's tips – make sure you think about how you package your viable option so that it speaks not only to the rational mind but the feelings associated. If he hadn't taken the step of getting the executive to experience what the patients were enduring every meal time, there's a whole crowd of people in that hospital would never have benefited just from a tiny tweak, and a little over $1000.

Are you conventional or 21st century?

Conventional teams no longer give us the characteristics needed for us to thrive in the 21st century. And even though we are in the second decade of the century, let's not kid ourselves that we have moved much from the 20th century paradigm of team.

CONVENTIONAL TEAMS	21st-CENTURY TRIBES
Capability	Learnability
Stability	Flexibility
Steadfast	Agile
Reactive	Proactive
Reads purpose	Lives purpose
Reads values	Lives values
Reputation driven corporate social responsibility	Authentic corporate social responsibility
Strategised to	Strategised with
Trusts slowly	Trusts quickly
HR pushed culture	Tribe owned culture
Output driven	Customer driven
Either/ or	And
Positional	Explorative
Operational	Operational and strategic
See ideas as overwhelming or too difficult	See ideas as opportunity
Avoid conflict	Step into robust ideological debate
Cooperate	Collaborate
Interact	Integrate
Default response is NO then shut down	Default response is YES then investigate
Feedback from superior	Multiple sources of feedback
Feedback - defend position	Feedback - growth
Performance development discussions	Ongoing growth discussion
Role description set in stone	Flexible role based on need
Problem	Challenge and opportunity
Default individual mindset	Deliberate tribe growth mindset
Individual capacity	Collective capacity
Contained learning	Messy learning
External accountability	Internal accountability
Run assumptions	Test assumptions
Competition as threat	Competition as opportunity to excel
Technology as burden	Technology as enabler

Glue

Michael Henderson, corporate anthropologist and organisational culture guru, has long used his extensive understanding and research of tribes to help leaders unlock the power of culture. His approach to thriving culture is three-faceted: Create a culture worth belonging to; have leaders worth following and do work worth doing. His books *Get Tribal: Simple, sound advice for understanding and improving workplace culture*, 2010 and *Chiefing Your Tribe: How to be a leader worth following*, 2012 are masterful observations of organisational culture and how to work deliberately on creating tribal cultures.

His perspective on some of the reasons that purpose and contribution are critical now is linked to the increase in choice and desire for meaning.

> We are in the 21st century, and unlike many generations who came before us who had little choice or resources available to them in regard to earning a living, meaningless work is now, in most people's aspirations, no longer acceptable. The meaning of work is for many employees now regarded as their second pay slip.
>
> Michael Henderson
> *Get Tribal! Simple, sound advice for understanding and improving workplace culture*

If we increase the collaboration and the learnability in our companies, it will create the culture for problem solving and innovation. We're responding to the needs of the customers, and the needs of the team. When people are strongly attached to purpose – momentum increases.

Imagine

In a majority of workplaces, people are committed to their jobs. They want to do the very best they can, but they have their heads down. They are being as great as they can be at the work that they're doing by themselves. Imagine the achievement if we were able to connect them more around their work. So many more ideas, so many more challenges approached with possibility. People working in different ways rather than the default way they've always worked. All because they're sharing their knowledge, sharing their approaches and their insights. That would lead to the environment where they're getting better outcomes, and they're focusing on what is it we are trying to achieve in our organisation. If we build the trust and connection between people, people will feel safer to interact at a deeper level. Rather than just talking about the footy on the weekend, then putting heads back down, they would have conversations around tricky projects, things that they're finding difficult, and inquiring about how someone else might approach the same issue. They would be learning better ways of doing things and co-creating future ways of working.

Trust

The connection to purpose and the creation of trust is a foundational part of the solution. If we don't get trust happening then we're fearful of the hard work, fearful of the hard conversations. We're unable to look at different ways of working. We're unable to contemplate the market competition without a sense of doom and gloom. 21st-Century Tribes look at their competition as opportunity to excel, whereas conventional teams look at the competition as a threat. Trust recodes desperation into great possibility. It's this turn of fear into reward that gives us the motivation to move.

Glue

Do some strategic reflection

To get anywhere close to having a thriving culture and strategy that will stand up to the changing context of the world and create the 21st-Century Tribes, the first step is to open up the conversation – to a collective reflection on where we are currently.

If purpose and trust are the critical intangibles of the glue that will get us there, conversation is the mixing agent that will enable it to set. Ask critical questions of your leadership team:

> What's holding us back from working in a faster/more creative/ more innovative/ collaborative/ streamlined/ high-achieving way? (whichever is most appropriate for you)

Look at what you do a with strategic eye, and ask:

> What could we do differently to get better outcomes?
>
> How should our teams operate to create a thriving environment of change?
>
> How do we help them to get there?

Next, go to the teams and ask the same question, followed by:

> What assumptions do we run around here about the way we work and what our customers need?
>
> How do we challenge our assumptions about the way we work?

It might be as simple as, 'We're not allowed to work in a different way.' It might be an assumption that says, 'Well, that's not my job, so I don't have a right to say anything about it'. 'We've done it that way for a long time, so it can't be changed.'

Never assume

A colleague of mine worked at with a team of the department of health looking to find better ways of helping people with mental health issues. They had all the senior leaders of the health department together. The workshop topic was 'What are the main challenges that are facing people suffering homelessness and mental health issues?' There was one person with lived experience, John, in the room, known as a 'consumer'. Consumers are often included in this type of forum to ensure the 'voice' of the particular group in focus.

As the discussion began, John pushed his chair away from the table and crossed his arms. Everyone else was working, noting down and discussing what they thought the main challenges were. He didn't contribute at all. The facilitator said, 'John, I noticed that you didn't put anything down or say anything. Do you care to share what is going on for you?' John replied, 'The day I take it upon myself to imagine what might be going on for other people is the day I give it all away'. The bureaucrats sat stunned, of course, and then said, 'How right – we are incredibly presumptuous not investigating that prior to this planning day.'

Conventional teams make many assumptions on behalf of others. 21st-Century Tribes are high in empathy – they understand the world of the customer and their collaborative partners, and they do it by asking questions, observing and often co-creating the solutions together.

Clue

Reflect on your customers

What's going on in your industry?

Are you aware of what's happening out in the world, and in the marketplace?

Do you know what trends are happening?

Do you know what best practice is?

Do you know what next practice is?

Are you creating an environment where you're looking at what can make the biggest change for your customers and what is going on out there?

Do you understand what your customers want?

Do you know what high-performance cultures that are sustaining this level of change and transformation are doing?

Tracey Ezard

Chapter Summary

Jump on and create the buzz.

The speed in which the world is moving needs us to work in a faster, smarter, and more connected way. Our increased capability and technology means that we can. It's time to get on with it or get left behind. It's time to tap into potential, and create an excitement in our organisational culture, so there's a great buzz about the work. Let's get on with it. We're on the inside watching the world outside change. We're getting left behind. The world needs us to be courageous and change the paradigm.

Imagine coming into work, and the conversations with people are buzzing about the work, keeping you in tune with all the great innovations they're trying, ways that they want to shift the status quo of how they work. People are excited about the vision and purpose, and they're committed to it. People are talking about what they are trying to achieve. There's a whole organisation approach to what you're trying to do and a real commitment to it. People are happy and engaged in their work. People are saying by default: ' How can I make this change happen?' and 'How can you help me to make this change happen?' People have been vested with the right to be able to make the place a better place, rather than sitting and saying, 'I have no control over this'. They've got influence over how they can do what they do in a better way.

What's next?

To be able to achieve this momentum, our first step is getting people out of their silos. If we have people sitting in their own worlds, looking at their work, and not seeing how it connects to each other, to the environment, and to the customer, we'll never get there.

The question is, are your people ready to accelerate and become 21st-Century Tribes, or do we need to smash some silos first?

2 Silos create stagnation

 Travel is fatal to prejudice, bigotry, and narrow-mindedness, and many of our people need it sorely on these accounts. Broad, wholesome, charitable views of men and things cannot be acquired by vegetating in one little corner of the earth all one's lifetime.

Mark Twain
The Innocents Abroad/Roughing It.

Sarah was excited about her new role. She was moving within her organisation to another team. The team she left behind was dynamic and exciting. She had learnt so much there and enjoyed the challenge of her role, but it was time to spread her wings. In her second role since university, she was ready to roll up her sleeves and co-create a dynamic and impactful campaign with the rest of the team. Her new team was rolling out a new service. Her job was to liaise with the team and with their stakeholders and craft the communication and marketing strategy. Sarah walked into the floor where her team worked with anticipation. It was a typical open-plan office with the conventional set up of cubicles with computer

Glue

terminals, and in the centre of every smaller cubicle hub, there was a round table with chairs. As she walked further into the area where her team was situated, her heart sank.

You might be able to imagine what Sarah saw that affected her so much. You probably know what you would be looking for, what you want to see and hear, and how you would want to feel.

For Sarah, people working together and interacting was a part of being in a dynamic team. They didn't live in each other's pockets. There was a balance of collaborating and people individually getting on with tasks. There was a constant energy of interaction, though. On the floor she had come from, if you gazed around, there would always be a few middle tables with a small group working together on something. In this new environment, she had just walked into there was a deathly silence. It was like the energy was sucked into a vortex. There was no speaking at all, anywhere. They all had their heads down over their terminals, grimly focused on the task at hand. For Sarah, unfortunately, things did not start looking up. Someone hurriedly looked up when she introduced herself and pointed her to a corner of the area where there were empty cubicles for her to sit down and get to work – by herself.

There's always a lot to learn when we step into a new role. There are new tasks to learn, processes to adhere to and new people to get to know. Then, we start getting attached to comfort – we know what the customer wants, we know how our boss wants us to deliver, and we have got the skills that will get the job done. Our drive to be in the learning space wains. Our expansion and growth slow as we feel more competent, on top of our jobs and the expectations upon us. And we start to stagnate. The comfort zone takes over, and we keep our head down.

The myth of the lifelong learner

There is a myth in many organisations that simply by being in the workplace we are growing, learning and getting better at what we do. We assume that time on the job also means we are growing our skills. But, unless we consciously create a learning environment in our teams, we become complacent and happy with the status quo. Improvement and innovation happens when people move out of comfort. In education, there is a slightly bitchy saying, 'How long have they been teaching? 20 years? Or one year, 20 times over?' But there is truth in it. The same applies in any field. We can be in the same cycle, applying the same thinking, doing the same activities in our little silo – and be happy doing it!

Have you ever travelled on a long-haul flight to another part of the world? Imagine getting to your destination jetlagged. You fall asleep in a dark room with heavy curtains drawn. With no alarm set, you sleep for a long period. You wake up, thinking it is daytime and get shocked as you draw the curtains and see that it is the middle of the night and you've slept through hours of the day and the evening. Individual silos work the same way; we assume that what is happening in the rest of the organisation and that the context is the same as it has always been. Unless we get out of our comfortable offices and away from our computer terminals, we're sleeping with the curtains drawn. We stay sitting in the status quo.

The status quo is dangerous.

The status quo is based on dangerous assumptions. It presumes that our context does not change, that clients' needs and expectations don't change. That technology, social media and globalisation do not have any effect on our part of the world.

Glue

When everyone puts their heads down to do the job, and no one looks up to see what is happening around them, it becomes our culture. Our own silos are the culprit – we set up little kingdoms of rare challenge. The work done and the thinking put into projects comes from one source – our own heads. We are ripe to fall into repetitive ways of thinking. Rather than being exposed to new ideas, expansive thinking, novel approaches, and ways of working we sit with our own theories about what works and our own knowledge.

And we stagnate, with little fresh thinking ever making it into our cubicles.

> Meetings, rather than being an opportunity for collaboration, are full of agenda items of the beige and boring.

Interactions with co-workers are transactional and focused on output rather than quality outcomes. Our default becomes status-quo thinking and comfort. We neutralise the 'lifelong learner' tag by 'this is the way we do things around here'.

As long as the people in organisation are working in silos, the business is prone to stagnation. It's an unpalatable truth, but once we realise that this is happening, we have a strategic focus for change.

Collaboration pokes at our comfortable assumptions.

When we sit in our silos, our assumptions about the way the world works become embedded. Our thinking is never challenged. We are focused more on 'me' and not on the client. We focus only on our part in the production line rather than our part of the whole service provided. We don't see ourselves as an integral piece of the whole picture.

When we challenge our assumptions, we activate our potential. And just like epoxy glue, Part A and Part B must combine to make it strong. More than one person coming together with purpose creates new ways of working that overcome our complacency.

In a recent Google survey, 73% of respondents agreed that their organisation would be more successful if employees could work in more flexible and collaborative ways. When asked, what changes would have the greatest impact on their organisation's overall profitability, 56% of respondents ranked a collaboration-related measure as the number one factor. This Google for Work survey, *Working Better Together 2015* also uncovered that collaboration and staff engagement are closely related, as discussed in Chapter One; engaged teams make collaboration and innovation much easier. Eighty eight per cent of respondents who strongly agreed that their company fosters a culture of knowledge-sharing and collaboration also strongly agreed that employee morale and job satisfaction are high.

Glue

Learning in silos

Companies who have an individual, siloed approach to training of people are pouring money down the drain. Historically, when leaders try to change performance, the default behaviour is to send individuals out to a course.

Money and time are being chewed up for several reasons:

20th century training methods

Many training programs are an exchange of information rather than transformative action learning. This is a hangover from an approach suited to the industrial age rather than the information age. An expert stands at the front of the room. Truths are spouted. Everyone writes copious notes, nods, and the trainer moves on. This antiquated approach to training rarely creates behaviour change and is full of the least evolved type of learning – transactional information exchange. High-quality training provides the opportunity for thought-provoking analysis and application to context.

Out of date trainers

Deadly, dull, snore-inducing trainers, who also work in silos, hate their jobs and the people they train. Nothing more needs to be said.

I'm back, and I'm excited! Now what?

Of course, there are great engaging trainers out there doing fabulous things. People come back to work inspired and excited about applying it back at work. The trouble comes when teams have no processes or rituals to share and explore how they can take the learning and embed it back into the workplace. Momentum fades and the inspiration wilts. In Fortune 500 companies, $31.5 billion is estimated to go down the drain on learning and development programs not transferring the learning back into the workplace, post course. (Source: 'Is Your Company Encouraging Employees to Share What They Know?' *Harvard Business Review*, November 2015.)

It's all about the individual, not the team

Individual capacity building is the only thing focused on, not team capacity. Learning not connected to the context of the team and the work needing to be done is limited in its effect. Building individual skills is critical for development. But if we never focus on capabilities the team needs for new initiatives, we get inconsistency.

It's learning and development's job

Leaders that outsource all the development of the team to the learning and development department are outsourcing part of their role.

> High collaboration means we solve problems together – and to do that, we need a strong learning focus in the team.

Glue

Your best people are looking for learning environments

Clients and employees are increasing their expectations of organisations. There is far more choice in the world now. People will vote with their feet, 'I'm not getting what I need, so I'm going elsewhere'. Clever innovators thinking outside the box are disrupting us. They are thinking more creatively than we are in mediocre organisations. They're working faster and more efficiently. Complacent organisations are missing the boat because they are not even thinking about moving faster. They're not looking outside. They're not creating an opportunity to reflect, 'How could we do this differently?' They just keep on doing what they're doing without thinking. Siloed and status quo organisations lose their best people. When team commitment to learning how to do things better and with purpose is missing, the best talent walks out the door. People who thrive on challenge and growth feel stifled by conventional teams who just co-exist. The spark of their natural social learning style becomes starved of oxygen. Engaged and motivated individuals tease ideas out, toss around perspectives and opinions and uncover hidden gems. It's the buzz of learning with each other for new solutions that excites them. Before the flame goes out completely, these clever people up and leave the business to find fulfilment elsewhere.

> CFO: But what if we develop our people and they leave?
>
> CEO: What if we don't and they stay?

Collaboration creates potential; silos dilute it

One of us is never as smart as all of us. No matter how brilliant our thinking is, we can always enhance it by throwing it in the ring with others. How do we create the culture to encourage a collaborative way of working?

Is history repeating itself?

I worked with a client recently whose organisation was failing. All the indicators that you would want to have in their context were not met. It was on a downward trajectory. The organisation was quite small and losing ground. I was brought in to work with them, co-creating their vision – how did they want to shift, what did they want to do differently? If they looked at themselves in 10 years' time what did they want to see?

As an important part of the process, they told the story of their journey. I was fascinated to hear what they had done and what they hadn't done. They'd worked in silos, and all did their own thing. They didn't learn from each other; they didn't challenge each other on how they could do things differently.

At the end, after we had shared the story, one woman, a long-term, committed employee of the company, saw in that moment how comfortable the status quo had become. 'Wow, have a look at 2008. We had our four-yearly organisational review in that year. It told us the same things that this review has just told. We took no notice, and we have spent eight years not doing anything about it. We've kept on doing the same thing that we were doing back then. Now, look at the problem we've got.'

Glue

Sitting in our own stew won't bring brilliance

When we connect our thinking and ideas with others, we end up with greater creativity in our approaches. We think in a less linear and more integrated way. Ideas that we wouldn't have thought of by ourselves are co-created with others. We start to realise that we don't have the best ideas. We like other people's ideas as well and begin to open our thinking. We spark off each other.

When we sit in our offices and try to figure things out with only our thinking to play with, we get stuck. Fear of looking like we can't do our job keeps us chained to the desk. Fear of judgement and failure hunches us down over our computer tapping away in an agony of uncertainty or confusion, rather than asking for someone else's opinion and help.

> Pockets of brilliance also stay hidden – someone who has the answer is sitting on it in their office, not letting anyone get it.

Because they never collaborate and connect with the team members or other people, their knowledge and skills never transfer. There is a power element to this. 'I'm good at what I do.' 'You may not be, but I am.' It creates an egocentric environment. True collaboration gets rid of an 'I' environment. People look at what they're doing to achieve success together, rather than one person being excellent at it and another not so great. Good ideas get fleshed out to be even better.

Don't just rinse and repeat

Eye rolling and comments of 'here we go again' occur when people are brought into a room to discuss what they need to do to 'fix' something. Mixed group tables are set up; discussion had. Everyone walks out and does the same thing they've always done. It's like being stuck on the rinse and repeat cycle in the washing machine. It might make us feel good at the time. We've all had a 'good honest' discussion about it. But it wasn't collaborating. Collaboration is about learning and action. It was just simply having a discussion. Frustration with the inaction festers. How could you change the wash cycle? It's always easier to get other people to change than ourselves. It's always easier to blame what's going on outside rather than, 'How am I contributing to this?' If none of us is modelling what we want to see in our teams, we'll never get it.

The true value of collaboration (and why it's different to dialogue)

Understanding that collaboration is more than discussion gives us the insight to look at what needs to change. We then question what actions will provide us with the greatest leverage to move this work forward. Don't just shuffle deck chairs, do some second-order change, not just first order change. First order change is moving things on the surface. Second order change is when we change beliefs about not only what we need to do but why. Many of us think we are at the pinnacle of collaborating when we are simply being cooperative. Before we get there, we might need to fight through some levels that are actively dissolving any glue of collaboration.

Glue

Corrosion

The solvent to collaboration is a corrosive environment. The definition of corrosion: the gradual destruction of materials by chemical reaction with their environment.

Have you ever walked into an environment that felt toxic? You feel it in the air. People don't even acknowledge each other. There seems to be no trust – in fact, there is often a profound sense of distrust.
A corrosive work environment is the home of the toxic workplace. In this space people of influence seem to be committed to creating an environment of fear and anxiety. In reality, they may not even be aware they are doing it. Their self-awareness may be low, and they do not have much empathy for others. Some may be fearful themselves, so their behaviours are those of 'survival of the fittest'. Whatever the underlying reasons, something major must shift. Only strong leadership and galvanising people towards a new vision of the future will fix it.

This corrosive stage can be an indicator of past, ineffective leadership. Some behaviours exhibited may be entrenched techniques from a fear based leadership regime. People then learn the behaviours of survival. Following are some of the hallmarks of the corrosive environment:

Fear

When fear is present, there is a genuine feeling of insecurity for many people on the team. They are afraid to speak their mind or voice their concerns. Fear also stands as a barrier to active experimentation and evaluation of new approaches to the work. There is just too much to lose for our personal safety and wellbeing. It's easier to stay with the status quo or retreat.

Unprofessional behaviour

Unchecked, unprofessional behaviour runs rife. People behave in inappropriate ways, but little has ever been done to address the actions or set clear expectations about what should be happening. There is little or no follow-up to underperformance. Professional standards are not articulated and embedded into the culture. When a team or organisation is in this corrosive space people do want it to be different; they are just too scared to speak up about it.

Feedback = conflict

At the corrosion stage any feedback about shifting behavior or approach is taken as personal attack. This is one of the biggest hurdles to move through as a team. Co-creating an environment of trust and collaboration, where people see feedback as a vital part of growth, appears a long way in the distance.

Lack of vision and innovation

The dreams and visions of the business are far from people's reality. There is a distinct lack of alignment of beliefs about the approach and how to enact it. Ideas and innovations are not in evidence, due to an unsafe learning environment for people to take risks, experiment or even give their opinions. The 'speaker for the opposition' seems to be the one heard most, actively sabotaging any forward momentum that anyone is trying to achieve. The result is good people leave and you are left with the ones who should leave!

Glue

Complacency

Complacency is the danger zone for any organisation. It creates a culture of 'near enough is good enough' where everyone is comfortably doing what they have always done. It's the stagnation point where our business is heading for oblivion if we don't do something about shifting the status quo.

The complacency zone has people I call 'leaners'. These people do the bare minimum. The behaviour can be hard to call because it just scrapes through as acceptable. It certainly doesn't create an environment of growth and momentum. People spend a lot of time leaning on the fence of comfort. They're happy with their little silo and happy to be left alone.

> This type of behaviour and culture is probably the topic leaders talk about the most when discussing the challenges of leading change.

The expected behaviours are not articulated, and there is not a strong focus on what a thriving culture is. The old premise of 'we do what we always have done' looms over new ideas and approaches that could shake up our results and increase our clients' satisfaction.

Do we see shift and transformation in the complacency zone? Not much. Any collaboration? Nah-uh.

Coordination and cooperation

The tokenistic collaborator is an expert in coordination and management. The terminology of collaboration is used but not enacted. Team members and stakeholder groups who are ready to be genuinely integrated into the work are not tapped into. The tokenistic collaborative leader still sees their role as the holder of knowledge and decider of strategies. They direct the group from a hierarchical position rather than partnership. The outcome is frustration and loss of purpose.

Co-creation and collective power

If you are a lover of Asian foods, you may have eaten dishes created with a master stock. Collaboration is like creating a master stock. The skills, experiences and 'corporate memory' of the staff who have been in the organisation for a long time are the foundations of the stock. For collaboration to be meaningful and fruitful there should be real valuing of what's gone before and how the journey of the organisation has created the now. But just as important, and adding to the complexity, is the addition of new team members, new experiences and expertise. Along with this comes new thinking by all involved. Collaborative teams understand how to carefully and lovingly stir these into the existing culture and build the depth and strength of the team.

> Collaboration is at its core
> all about learning.

Steps to take

Once we understand the levels of collaboration, we can diagnose where we need to step up. We identify disconnection that is occurring due to silos. We identify pockets of excellence and pockets of underperformance and how to use collaboration to increase the team's capacity. We start to understand where our client's needs are not being fulfilled. Chapter Five takes a deep dive into the levels of collaboration. Here are some first steps you can take:

Talk about the possibilities

Have an initial conversation with your teams specifically on what possibilities they see in collaborating altogether. Where are their intersections? Most people in teams would easily identify where they could work better together. Sometimes it's the systems or culture that stops them. Often the team just hasn't been strategic about making it happen, and if it happens, it's by chance.

Has collaborating worked for you?

As a team, share personal stories of times where you have worked with other people in a rewarding, collaborative way. What was the circumstance? What were the outcomes? What was in place that helped that to happen?

Tracey Ezard

Chapter summary

When we work by ourselves, we don't have much fun. But working together with others brings out the best in ourselves.

If we don't work together, we stagnate. And when we don't tap into others we miss out on learning their wisdom and sharing our own.

Imagine reaching the pinnacle of what's possible with the team because the glue of the team means that you are working for each other's success. The work environment is positive, energetic. The team is focused on working together for the success of the team. You've realised how to unlock potential. You see the gaps, and you're working purposefully to get them solved. Your team is working with you, and thriving because they are doing so. The challenge and the opportunity to get better is driving them.

What's next?

In the next chapter, we're going to look at the shift of leadership that is required to build the bonds and lift us out of convention. A leadership approach that relegates a power over approach to the bin, and moves to creating transformation with their teams. We need leaders that can build relationships and culture just as much as hitting whatever measures the company uses to define success.

3 from territorial to transformational leadership

When leadership shifts, cultures shift

If we don't create the change we want in ourselves, no change will appear in others. When leaders don't change behaviour and the beliefs driving them, the momentum will not arrive. The old version of leadership is from a military paradigm, and it's a 'power over' paradigm. Unfortunately, many leadership development courses still hark from this military principle. It makes hierarchy the modus operandi, which says the further up the hierarchy I am, the more powerful I am, and the more important – even brilliant my contribution is.

> This is flawed thinking in today's age. Leadership education that does not seek to develop collaborative skills is contributing to continued silos and lack of innovation.

Command and control, and a presumption that the strategic thinking we need only happens in the chief executive suite, will keep us in the status quo. The guiding belief is, if we don't tell people what to do, they'll have no *idea* what to do. The archaic and erroneous belief that our people don't know how to work more effectively is misguided with today's savvy workforce.

Territorial leadership often accompanies command and control. It postures: 'This is my patch, so do as I say'. This old paradigm is not getting engagement, buy in or traction. Territorial leaders create silos through the protection of turf. Most importantly, the great cross-team thinking that we need for the future shuts down. The collaboration we need for transformation and future success doesn't occur when someone is fortifying the silo.

When leadership shifts, cultures shift. Then, we're able to get extraordinary results. Carolyn Taylor, author of *Walking the Talk: Building a culture for success*, 2005, and one of the world's leading expert in culture says, 'Significant culture change can only occur when the behaviour and the mindset of the top team changes'. If the power base of traditional leadership doesn't shift, organisational change will not. Command and control are winning out rather than tapping into the wisdom, the brilliance, and the potential of the people within the whole organisation.

To achieve change in leaders we need be learners. A space of discomfort pushing us to change rather than just expecting others to change is a good thing. We need to be aware of default habits that continue behaviours keeping power, command and control as our driving principles. That first step of self-awareness and self-reflection is critical. Always start within.

Why should I?

If leadership won't change with the times the talent leave. Great leaders create an environment where people want to work with us. They don't have to, they're not coerced into it; they seek to work with us. Whether it as a project-worker or as a long-term employee, great talent is drawn to leaders who bring out potential.

Leading from the middle

Some of you reading this chapter will not be in the senior part of your organisation but passionate about leadership and creating a thriving collaborative environment. If you are, then I encourage you always to change yourself first. I've worked with many middle leaders downhearted because they've gone to senior leaders, excited to do things in a more collaborative, co-creating way, only to be shut down. It can be easy for middle leaders to feel frustrated about the lack of insight at the top level. The senior leaders seem unable to recognise that their behaviour is shutting down innovation, creativity and engagement. This can be exhausting and distressing.

Where can you impact?

My advice is, start with your circle of influence as a middle leader. Where can you make the most difference? It may be the interactions between your team and other teams. Increase collaborative opportunities that have positive impact wherever you can. As your influence and your success grow, then you have more confidence to leverage your influence upward. Compassion is important for leaders at any level to help influence change. Enhancing empathy upwards instead of embracing the frustration of the situation might get surprising results. It moves us from victim into an influencer.

Glue

21st-Century Tribes are full of influencers. People are in their power and feel that they can shift things. It's critical for middle leaders to feel like that.

> Middle leaders can be some of the most disfranchised in organisations. To see that they can influence through their behaviours is an empowering step.

Growth

William is a senior director in a growing organisation, and his team fared quite well in a cultural survey. The overall organisational result was abysmal – even within their sector, which historically scores badly on culture surveys. William's area fared a lot better. Still room for improvement, but higher than the rest of the organisation.

The organisation displayed behaviour consistent with abuse of power, working in silos, passive-aggressive behaviour, and avoiding challenges. Customers were miserable with the service, teams felt disengaged and the morale across the whole place was rock bottom. The year before, a reputable consultancy put in place a major leadership program. The senior executive assumed that there would be changes in the results because of that leadership program. There was little. William's colleagues in the executive team couldn't work out why they were achieving these dismal results. They assumed because they had all done the training, something would shift.

Having worked with William's senior team for some years, I knew why his large team had fared better. In fact, William's response to the rest of the executive team displayed why. When they mentioned to him how happy he must be with his team, he said, 'I am proud of what we've achieved, but I won't be happy until we show improvement across the whole organisation. Until we've done that, I know there's still more work to do'.

William is a 'we' leader. He believes in creating a connection that runs right through the organisation, not just within teams. Until he and his colleagues create that desired environment company-wide, he's not prepared to say that his work is done.

William also has high emotional intelligence. He's committed to his team having authentic input in discussion about how they can continue to improve and get better at what they do.

William's team reflected on their specific results. They looked at what type of behaviour should be strengthened, and what developed. Even with the good results, they knew that some of the middle leaders were not rising to their potential or feeling fulfilled and engaged. William and his team had a constructive robust discussion on their contribution to those results. Together, they created strategies that focused on building the potential of the middle leaders. The team challenged each other to keep trialing new ways of leading, taking on board the feedback they had received.

William and his team are 'learners'. They've invested in developing their emotional intelligence and their reflection as a group on what they're trying to achieve with their leadership. They see their learning and leadership development as a critical strategy to their success. They've also worked on how they collaborate. They strategise and action breaking down any silos that they can identify within their teams. They work in a siloed organisation. William's teams always ask: 'Where are our integrations? What are our partnerships? Where is it that collaboration is critical?' They reflect on how they can influence the business-wide silos and work at breaking them down through relationships and positive working collaborations.

The other executives at William's level had gone back to default behaviour after their leadership training. The training didn't challenge the set beliefs and assumptions about leadership among participants enough for change. They didn't increase dialogue with the next tier down as William had done. They didn't seize the learning opportunity to build a strong connection to the middle leaders and bring them into conversations about creating real change. They all went back to their silos and their default 'I' behaviours in their teams.

They also didn't move enough to a 'we' mindset as a senior executive team. One of their biggest goals is to improve collaboration within the organisation, as it's fortified with strong concrete like silos. They failed to commit as a group to changing their own behaviours. The conversations, goals and actions they needed to change were not undertaken during, and after that rigorous training as senior leaders, and middle leaders. Default behavior crept back in.

Why won't they just do it?

It is easy for us to assume that if leaders direct people to collaborate, they just get on with it. Conventional wisdom says it's the team that needs to work differently, not the leader. Get someone in to do some 'teambuilding', and all our problems will be solved. Collaboration is a difficult gig to get used to, especially if the culture of the organisation is based on territorialism and 'looking out for my patch'. People, in general, want to work together. Often stronger power plays are going on above them. Leaders direct people to work together more collaboratively, then their own behaviour gets in the way, and hierarchy shuts people down and back into their burrows.

Partnership, not hierarchy

The paradox here, of course is that the very nature of being told to work collaboratively is against the principle of co-creation and collaboration. Leaders need to drop hierarchical behaviours to be able to collaborate properly. When we lose the need to be more powerful, we move towards partnership. We lose the military identity paradigm of leadership, the need to be right, and we drop our ego. To become a collaborative and transformative senior leader, the first place to collaborate is in the boardroom with our peers, and that's where most territorialism occurs. Decrees come from the senior teams wanting more partnership, and collaboration. You walk into a high-level meeting and the same people are having turf wars with each other.

Forget the easy road

It's always easy to tell other people to change rather than ourselves. We're not okay with discomfort. We're not very good at doing things differently. There's a vulnerability when trying new things that we fear. Leaders are prone to putting up a mask of invulnerability. The general expectation of leaders is that they shouldn't make mistakes. Leaders should know the answers, and any sign of not knowing is a weakness. This makes us more reluctant to put ourselves in a learning mode to shift.

Lead the learning

We often don't make time for self-reflection and self-awareness. Leadership teams I work with often reflect, at the end of intense discussion about leading, how little they take the time to do it. For forward-thinking 21st Century Leadership tribes, it's a critical and frequent conversation.

If we turn this reflective conversation into a leadership ritual, it encourages us to think differently about what are we doing. We have more collaborative learning conversations with our colleagues. We start asking learning questions of each other: 'How are we challenging ourselves to do things differently? What is a strong, clear signal to the organisation that we are wanting and willing to change, transform and learn?' Chapter Six offers further insights on how to create a collaborative learning environment.

Stop saying, 'Don't come to me with a problem, come to me with a solution'.

I hear leaders saying this all the time. We need to stop it. It's a great way to shut down any hope of our team working through solutions *with* us. Soon, after this type of reaction, people retreat from coming to us at all to brainstorm new ideas, or chew the fat over a particular problem. We reinforce hierarchy. Leadership stays as an unapproachable authority, rather than a partner in the creation process. Teams thrive when they are certain their leaders are open to co-create solutions with them when required. Leaders who are willing to say: 'Come to me solution-focused and let's talk about it' are building environments where innovation can thrive.

Tracey Ezard

Territorial to Transformational Leadership

TERRITORIAL	TOKENISTIC	COLLEGIATE		COLLABORATIVE	TRANSFORMATIONAL
Siloed	Traditional	Conventional	TEAM	High Performing Team	21st-Century Tribe
Power, ego driven coercion	Words of collaboration, actions of Silos	Harmony and ease; comfort	DEFAULT	Momentum and productivity	Creativity, innovation
Winners and losers	Frustration in team and partners	Comfortable thinking	OUTCOME	Partnerships	Collective capacity
Leadership driven	Consults for appearance sake	Cooperative, seeks input	PROBLEM SOLVING	Co-creation with team and others	Flexible. Most appropriate strategy for situation
Distrust	Cynicism, scepticism	Uncertainty	TRUST	Trust	High trust

→ TRUST
→ COLLABORATION

Glue

The territorial leader

When we're in a territorial state, there is toxicity. Fueled by power plays and ego, full-on sabotage and active resistance by leaders plays out. Major distrust and poor behaviour go along with it. Individual agendas outweigh the collective. Rules of engagement are poor, vague and not stuck to. Territorial leaders are about protection of self, rather than the good of 'we'. This is portrayed as being protective of their team, but the base value that is driving that behaviour is a strong self-interest. When a territorial leader is in charge, the potential that people bring to teams is not used or valued. Competition rather than collaboration connects people's work, so it's a dog-eat-dog competitive environment, to the detriment of a better outcome.

Territorialism happens when leaders bunker down with their teams and look with suspicion at other parts of the organisation. The combative language metaphors used are from battle mentality: 'We need to bunker down', 'protect our budget or project', 'I'm going in to fight for resources', 'no other team is going to get the run on us'. It reflects division at the highest level, not cohesion or common purpose. Moves towards collaboration are stymied by strong barriers and systems. Systems and decisions that encourage silos are the norm. Teams don't align to the whole organisational strategy, just to their own.

These are some of the challenges that William and his team encounter when working with other parts of their business. Decisions made impact them without any communication or collaboration. People assigned to work with them on partnership projects are pulled off without any discussion, due to their leader deciding they are needed elsewhere. Experts in one area of the business don't see the need to tap into anyone else's expertise because 'they have all the answers'.

Strategic links between teams aren't explicit, and are not leveraged to get better outcomes. Communications levels in a territorial phase are limited and guarded in nature and distrust drives them.

The tokenistic leader

Mike is a senior leader who sees himself as a great collaborator. He recently held a one-hour meeting with 35 people, saying he wanted to get their opinions, ideas and insights on a challenging issue. Starting off by declaring this intention, he then started talking *at* the group for 47 minutes about his thoughts, ideas and insights. That left 18 seconds each for everyone else. Mike believes himself to be collaborative – but his actions don't show that. In fact, the people in the room would say the main belief that drives Mike is that he knows the answers. Many of them left the room reasonably sure they had just been part of a tokenistic hat tip to consultation and collaboration.

The tokenistic collaborative leader is great at coordination and management. They have all the terminology of collaboration. But the terminology has arrived far before the behaviour. Team members and stakeholder groups who could be included and asked their opinion are not accessed. All that intelligence is wasted. The concept of co-creation is unknown territory. Co-creation is when we all come together to make something more that we could have created alone. This concept is drawn out further in the chapters ahead. The tokenistic leader sees their role as the holder of knowledge and the decider of the strategies. 'I run the show.' They direct the group from a hierarchical position rather than partnership. The outcome for the team and others is frustration and a loss of purpose.

Glue

Transformative leadership – moving from convention

Deciding to be more collaborative leaders starts with easy steps. Moving beyond being collegiate, we push to challenge the status quo. We meet strategically and purposefully on the operational challenges of silos within the organisation. We draw our discussions back to our purpose and increase the conversation around collaboration. We redesign systems that are blocking collaboration. Discussion and activity centre on working together and designing the quality and the thinking behind the work. We focus on working together as a senior team to co-create better ways of working.

For leadership teams who move to this space, there's a culture of inclusion and collective purpose. Rather than having all the answers, we are open to others' ideas. Opportunity for idea generation, innovation and trialing is the norm of this environment. Conflict as an attack isn't in evidence. What happens instead is great, robust ideological debate. It's about respectful and professional conflict to unearth the best ways to work. We bring people in that have got the knowledge and passion that we need to move to our goals. It's a thriving place that challenges thinking, and where leaders are open to learning.

Mistakes are opportunities to fine tune and learn. People from different disciplines take the advantage of listening and learning from each other to innovate and problem solve, and the client is always at the centre. The focus is on the customer as the main driver to change. The collaborative leader fosters the environment for working together. Together these leaders become transformational for the organisation. They develop people and themselves. It's a place of learning and growth. No longer are the yearnings for collaboration from the teams squashed, they are nurtured.

Looking inward – testing our beliefs

As a leadership team, reflect on these questions. Challenge each other's thinking.

Does our leadership team believe in the power of the collective?

Do we want a collaborative culture in this team?

Do we believe that diversity is a strength or a weakness?

How can we create an environment where we're nurturing and strengthening a collaborative culture?

What is our default behaviour when diverse opinions are raised?

Do we believe that other people's opinions are valid and valuable?

How do our behaviours display that belief?

If we invalidate people, shutting people's conversation down when they don't agree with us, then our beliefs are saying the opposite.

If we don't test these beliefs out, we're not going to change behaviour. Belief conversations are discussions many leadership teams don't have. Behaviours and relationships create culture. These discussions help us to be mindful of our actions and values. Being mindful leaders is critical if we want people to do extraordinary work. The inward space of reflection and self-awareness is stop number one. Stop number two is having the conversation as a leadership team.

Glue

Be open to feedback

If we believe that we have all the answers, then collaboration is difficult. When my business manager, Suzie, first started working with me, I found it a challenge. As a collaboration expert, I create environments for collaboration with my clients every day. But being in my own business for over a decade, I had always done my work my way. There was no one else to bounce off, co-create with, or ask for their opinions! In our first few weeks together, I had to become aware of, and change, my default behaviour. I believe without reservation that, by opening my thinking to embrace Suzie's approaches and ideas, both of us benefit and work better. This is the purpose that drives my business – to help teams and leaders create thriving environments where extraordinary work happens. My past roles in organisations were built on collaboration and learning. Co-creating with my teams and building capacity had been one of the joys of working within a business. But I had settled into being a one-woman band; that was clear when I started working with Suzie.

> Unintentionally, after a decade of working in the office by myself, I had developed all sorts of default behaviours.

I remember on one day early on in our working relationship, Suzie challenged an idea I had about a client. She proposed another (much better) way of thinking about this client. And it hurt! I felt threatened. 'I am supposed to have all the answers in my business,' said the little voice in my head. 'Aren't I the expert? You've only been here five minutes; how would you know a better way to do things?'

As an educator, I know that whenever discomfort and threat are rising in my body and mind, I am in a learning zone. We have a choice when our ideas feel threatened.

We can step into it and take the feedback and explore further, or go on the defensive and shut down the conversation.

That was a pivotal experience for me. I want to create a vibrant, collaborative culture in my team; I need to get out of default thinking and behaviour.

Suzie and I have shifted to constructing our goals in partnership. Instead of me coming up with plans on how to approach on the big goals of our business, we co-create our strategy. Rather than me plotting an approach by myself and presenting it, we brainstorm together. As an intelligent and skillful professional, Suzie brings insight and ideas that I don't have, and when we mix our thinking together, we come up with the best path forward.

Inward beliefs → outward behaviours

Wayne was quite devastated because he'd been given feedback by a trusted colleague that he had been talking over the top of some of his female peers. He was upset because he thought he was too mindful to do that. He had spent time building his facilitation skills in ensuring that everyone had a voice. He started to allocate time to look at himself from above, the 'meta' position; he realised the criticisms were true. His default behaviour of talking over the top of the women in the room came through when it was something that he was passionate about. It was this first step of discomfort and feedback that allowed him to grow and change his behaviour. He spent time soul-searching into his beliefs about contributions from females and felt a huge shift to some default beliefs he had. He realised that he believed that his opinion was more important than the females in the room. It was his inward focus on his thinking and feeling and the realisation on his impact that created the outward shift he needed.

When we connect our outward behaviours to our inward beliefs, we can facilitate collaboration. Our behaviours become about building trust, being open to feedback. As leaders, we then facilitate great, robust discussion. We become okay when opinions are challenged. We realise that beliefs of being right, leadership command and control and power undermines true collaboration. We unearth differences and nonalignment to provoke and challenge thinking. Non-alignment is where we find innovation. If we don't create the environment where we can have robust debate, and sit in ambiguity, we don't get collaborative perspective. We get head nodding and blind agreement.

Strategic development of leaders as collaborators is a step in the right direction for companies who want to challenge silos and default thinking. Increasing collaborative leadership will increase trust, buy-in, and commitment. It brings a safe environment for people and greater creativity and innovation. It starts with leaders courageous enough to be vulnerable and not have all the answers. Brene Browne has become a global thought leader on the topic of vulnerability after her first Ted Talk – The Power of Vulnerability – and writing several books subsequently. As a social researcher, Browne has identified that the quality that holds us back from connecting and being authentic is shame and an unwillingness to be vulnerable. She sees vulnerability as 'the birthplace of creativity, innovation and change'. In her latest book, *Rising Strong*, she says, 'Vulnerability is not weakness, it's our greatest measure of courage.' I encourage you to delve into Brene Browne's views on vulnerability.

Steps

Individually write down the key beliefs you hold about leadership and then share them as a group. Discuss how they drive the behaviours people experience from this team. Ask a further question: What are our fundamental beliefs about collaboration? What are our core beliefs on how we work together? Then have tough conversations around where you see the beliefs in evidence and when do you not see them in evidence? What is it that you do as a leadership team that is counter to these beliefs? Are they holding you back from your goals? What are other beliefs that would serve you better? What behaviours would you see coming out of them? How could you hold each other accountable?

Here are a few examples of collaborative beliefs:

> Better ideas come from collective thinking.
>
> Not one of us is as smart as all of us.
>
> Challenging each other's thinking is our role.
>
> Discomfort means learning.
>
> Diversity gets better solutions.
>
> Never assume.

Chapter summary

Leaders are the master architects of silos, so they also need to detonate them.

Territorial leadership corrodes trust. Imagine if as a leader you create an environment that finds challenge and collaboration exciting. Imagine if your senior leadership team are as committed to collaborating with each other as they want their people to be. Imagine if they were willing to change just as much as the whole organisation needs to change. Every level of the organisation would feel real connection and galvanisation around purpose. It would be a true 21st-Century Tribe, led by connected leaders buying into the need to behave in a different way.

What's next?

Let's next look at some of the key elements of the glue required for the momentum and collaboration required for the 21st century. What creates the cohesiveness to do extraordinary work?

Our first stop is how we approach the big question of where should you focus to create transformation. Strategy or culture? Do you have a strategy team that never talks with the culture team? Why do culture and strategy sit in their silos? Is it contradictory that they are siloed when the need to collaborate culturally and strategically is a focus for survival in the future?

Part II

The Glue of Collaboration

Strategy

Culture

Learning

4

Culture and strategy should eat breakfast together

Culture eats strategy for breakfast.

This quote, which is questionably attributed to organisational development expert Peter Drucker, gets many a head nodding in a room when mentioned. It highlights the reality that if we focus on only the nuts and bolts of strategy rather than the people side of business we are heading for a big FAIL. With the important issues of engagement, well-being and motivation levels impacting on organisational success, culture is the critical component that brings strategy to life. It builds the social capital that enables people to do great things together.

Culture and strategy = professional capital

Michael Fullan and Andy Hargreaves, giants of the education world, have drawn on an extensive body of research in the education sector to identify what is it that makes schools and school systems highly effective.

Much of this is attributed to what they label 'Professional capital'. The insights and research outlined in *Professional Capital – Transforming*

Glue

Teaching in all Schools, 2012, is just as applicable to businesses with knowledge workers. Intellectual collaboration is critical to success wherever knowledge is the basis of our offering.

'Professional capital' is the overarching term under which three different types of capital interact. These terms are used in many industries. It is the combination of the three that is of significant insight for us in the journey to extraordinary outcomes.

Human capital

Social capital

Decisional capital

'Human capital' is the individual human smarts that people bring to our teams – it is the 'talent of individuals'. Social capital is the collaborative power of the group. 'Decisional capital' is 'the wisdom and expertise to make sound judgments about learners that are cultivated over many years'.

Replace the word *'learners'* with whatever is pertinent to your circumstance. It could be *'marketing' 'product development' 'telecommunications' 'risk management'*.

It's the interweaving of these three capitals that creates professional capital. In research that Hargreaves and Fullan cite within their book, schools with high human capital and high social capital show the biggest impact on students. Interestingly, schools with lower human capital and high social capital often fared better than schools with only high human capital. Social connection and collaborative work impacts more on outcomes than having brilliant teachers doing their own thing.

Social capital creates the culture and collaborative capability. Human capital identifies individual capability. Decisional capital is the ability to judge. Professional capital combines all three capitals to make the wisest decisions – not created in a vacuum, but with the insight and ideation of the whole organisation – co-created strategy that draws from a variety of sources and robust exploration of future directions.

Being a learning company – what can education tell us?

High-quality education systems set up expert collaborative learning systems for their teachers. They create deep collaboration and learning environments. Their work is relentlessly evaluated. They give peer-to-peer feedback and strive to continuously increase the level and quality of their impact on students. And alongside all other sectors, the shifting paradigm of the world needs them to ensure 21st century skills such as sense-making, collaborative problem solving, data analytics and digital literacy are crafted alongside the more traditional skills of literacy and numeracy. High-quality education environments support and build the collective capacity of their teachers to be able to meet the demands required of them.

For many other industry sectors, much of this rigour and deep learning is far out of their league. Learning companies are the key to future success. Companies that encourage people to be learners and unearth ways of doing things in a different way create environments of development and growth – not stagnation. When we build this growth environment, culture and strategy both win.

Glue

> The reality is strategy and culture shouldn't be seen in separate camps. Co-creating the strategy of the organisation *with* our people has a huge effect on the cultural side of things.

We tap into one of the most vital ways to strengthen people's engagement and a sense of purpose: increased voice and recognition of the value they bring.

If we insist on strategy only being developed and shaped by leaders or the 'strategic development team' with no input from the people doing the work, we end up with words on a page that people ignore. Strategy created by a few individuals in a closed room won't build the momentum we need for success. When people are dissatisfied with their work environment and disengaged, it's not just about how they get along. They're quite often dissatisfied with the amount of input they have. They dislike the lack of control over their work. Little or no ability to have any influence over the direction of the organisation and things that are not working frustrates. Companies are full of onerous and disconnected systems. Overflowing with paperwork and administrivia that doesn't add value to doing *the work*. (Administrivia – a made up word that beautifully describes the trivial administrative tasks and agenda topics that take most of the time people spend together.)

We rush from meeting to meeting overwhelmed with the small things. We don't have time to talk about what we are passionate about. We forget to talk about purpose, and we forget to value people for the skills they bring. Our people don't get much input into strategy and the way the organisation works. The vision of many businesses is done like a 'set and forget' step, put up on the wall and never mentioned again.

Buy-in

Co-create strategy and vision with people in your organisation and give them a voice. You will see an increase in buy-in and commitment as soon people are charged within the teams to take the work forward. This level of engagement builds a culture of connection and trust with people. We can make the wisest decisions about future strategy when we have gone back to root purpose together and started there. Why is it we're doing this? For what purpose? What is it we need to do to get us there?

Then robust conversations about tactics and operational issues become possible. We are all committed to the same higher purpose. We become more committed to how to work better together. An essential part of our strategy should always include how we work as a team or how we work as an organisation. Don't leave this sort of cultural work to chance – embed it in strategic directions.

Committing to action

Articulating and committing to the purpose and our loftier vision brings everything into alignment. We can challenge our thinking on how we might be able to achieve it. Rather than just look at tasks, think about the behaviours that will drive the work.

> How should we work to succeed?
>
> What does success look like?
>
> How do we interact and collaborate in a way that leads to success?
>
> What behaviours will get us the required goals?

Glue

Winning over the sceptics

Kate is a client of mine who became the CEO in an organisation where she had been a senior leader at a time when people had their heads down just doing their jobs. Committed to what they were doing, committed to their clients, but doing it in a siloed and disconnected fashion. As an organisation, they had been surviving – just. Morale was low. It was stressful, and they weren't performing well. Kate was trying to get them to innovate and do things differently. She wanted to create a connection to the bigger vision.

To start with, Kate brought her middle- and senior-leadership teams together. This crew were huge sceptics of the process to start with. They looked with suspicion at the agenda, sure it would be a waste of time. Cynics in the group did not believe the senior team wanted to hear from them at all. They saw it as a 'check the box exercise'.

From 'I' to 'we'

We needed to begin with the middle and senior leaders. The rest of the staff were not on board at all with setting a new course for the future. The most influential of them felt safe with the status quo. It was easy and comfortable, even if they were not very engaged or happy. For many of us, known unhappiness and mediocrity is a preferable option to unknowns and ambiguity. Some were attached to their power base in the old order.

The senior and middle leaders were critical to win over in this first conversation. They would help to build momentum back in the workplace. In the beginning, there were a lot of people in the room thinking, here we go, this will just be a talk fest. It was important we had the environment that built a culture of collaboration and a culture of strategic thinking. This retreat was the first step.

We tracked the story of the organisation and where they had come from. We discussed the environmental context pushing down on them from outside, which was quite intense. Customers and regulators expected them to change and improve, which was reasonable, but felt like a huge pressure.

We mindfully created a safe environment with open and candid discussion about the current state of the organisation. Then we looked to the future. The team asked questions of each other:

>Where is it we want to head?
>
>What is our vision?
>
>What is it we're trying to achieve?

We metaphorically painted the picture of that and created a compelling vision that articulated where they wanted to go. Good, robust conversations ensued that wasn't personal. It was all about the vision, all about the organisation. Pure, simple conversation:

>What's going on?
>
>Where is it that we're going wrong or stalling?
>
>What are the systems and behaviours stopping us?
>
>Culturally, what's stopping us?'

When we were having the conversations, people starting seeing each other in a different light. They realised they all had the same intent. They had positive commitment to the organisation and what they were all trying to do. Neuroscience says when we see people in a light that's like our own, we feel more connected to them. When we can see people are not just saying, 'This is what I believe,' but, 'This is what I'm prepared to discuss,' we build trust.

Glue

When we are open to influence, we are more trusting of each other. Rather than, 'I'm right,' we realise we are here to solve this problem together. It starts to shift the culture naturally. It moves it from an 'I' perspective to a 'we' perspective – we're in this together.

Having strategic conversations about our vision looks at not only the strategic work we need to do, but also the belief and behaviour change we need to make. We bring culture and strategy naturally together in the conversation. This approach brings commitment and buy-in. Getting team-oriented about why are we here and what our goals are builds committment. How we need to behave to reach these goals is the cultural question. Four years later when Kate's team came to design their new strategy, they had moved from a disconnected organisation to one that was aligned in both the way they worked and where they were heading. They felt they had moved from 'surviving' to 'thriving'. When we connect people and purpose together, we get momentum.

More than just a pay packet

The *Deloitte Millennial Survey 2016* shows purpose and happiness in their work drive millennials. They want to be connected to the bigger why. They also want to understand how their parts fit and expect to enjoy their job. For millennials, they won't stick around. There's more flexibility in their approach and willingness to go elsewhere. They also want environments where learning is encouraged and built into the DNA of the organisation. Their potential is tapped into and built, and their development is important. Many people not in the millennial category also want this!

In 'The Power of Meeting Your Employees Needs', *Harvard Business Review*, November 2014, Tony Schwartz and Christine Porath, share the four core needs for employees uncovered through a survey of more than 12,000 employees. The study identified that employees are more satisfied and productive if these are met:

Renewal – opportunities to renew and recharge at work

Value – feeling valued for contributions

Focus – being able to concentrate on important tasks and the control for when and where to get them done

Purpose – doing more of what they do best and enjoy being connected to a higher purpose at work.

Further meta-analysis of 263 research studies across 192 companies showed that employers with the most engaged employees were 22% more profitable than those with the least engaged employees.

How much time do you put into meeting these needs?

How do we need to BE to achieve these goals?

The conventional wisdom is culture eats strategy for breakfast. Right on – if you do not have the culture, you can have the greatest strategy in the world, and not have anyone enact it. But co-create the strategy together, you'll get rock stars. People will work together to create the vision.

The culture eats strategy for breakfast metaphor resonates for many people who have sat in strategy meetings being bored to snores, creating strategy that never gets looked at again, or looked at just in time for performance measurement reviews. Or being in a team that is just told to get on with it, rather than having a strategic discussion on how they might achieve their goals.

Glue

The outdated military leadership paradigm discussed previously doesn't fit what we need in the world today. I'll set the strategy. You simply do it. We have got bright, savvy people working for us. We need to tap into them, their potential, and get them thinking about what we need to do rather than just the leaders 'knowing' it all.

One of us is never as smart as all of us

People make strategy work. Let's not underestimate what is possible when we work in the nexus between culture and strategy. Elevating our teams to a strategic mindset creates a culture of growth and excellence. It sets the glue we need to thrive.

Building strategy and culture together is about cultivating conversations that connect people to purpose and people to people. Then we can also focus on meeting our customers' needs.

Strategic intelligence at all levels

The process of co-creating strategy is an integral part of the glue of 21st-Century Tribes. Let's define strategy. Strategy is not just the high-level directions of the organisation, set down by the Board or Executive. It's also what do we do as a team. Where are our big picture goals that give us the momentum we need for success? It's asking, 'What is our commitment and action?'

Every level of an organisation should have their own strategy. Even when you have a business plan to operationalise, being strategic about how you're doing it is critical. Co-created strategy is like an electrical circuit. When a company co-creates a strategy, the teams in the organisation feed in their perspectives, reflections, data and ideas. What is our point of view? What is our vision of the future? This circuit feeds into the central solenoid of the strategy creation, whatever that may be – the Board or senior team. It is even more robust when all of those levels discuss the issues with each other. The flow of energy in a circuit is a continuous loop. It does not work if any part of the circuit is not connected.

Don't socialise strategy after it's been written. Craft it collaboratively while it's being co-created. Conventional organisations 'socialise' strategy after the senior executives have created it. Those on the ground are told what the strategy is in a whiz-bang gala unveiling, with little or no input into the contents. It cascades down. In a 21st-Century Tribe organisation, the flow is up and down, with constant feedback loops that go through it. The right people need to drive the co-creation of the strategy. And by that, I mean people who know how to collaborate. Not a strategic development team who have no idea how to empathise and understand the opinion and perspectives of anyone other than themselves.

This model of strategic collaboration is us doing it together. Processes are in place that allow for input, creativity and innovation to be included, not dismissed. Leadership provides the time and opportunity for teams to step up and think more strategically. The right questions just need to be asked. It's not about hierarchy; it's about partnership.

Glue

Give voice – gain value

One way to strengthen people's engagement and sense of purpose is an increased voice. If leaders or the strategic development team shape the strategy without input, we end up with words on a page that people ignore. If a few individuals in a closed room develop strategy, the momentum we need for success is not created. When we give people a voice in the direction and desired future, commitment and engagement grows. We increase the value our strategy when our teams come together to do the work. It is no longer a dusty few pages in a folder. Or in a file on the share drive no one reads.

I have heard many comments over the years bringing culture and strategy together that show both approaches:

> *We just get edicts from on high – we have no idea why.*
>
> *We just get into something and yet again it changes – with no real reason that we know of.*
>
> *I have some great ideas for the new initiative I want to share, but there is no forum for me to do it in.*
>
> *I don't feel REALLY listened to – listening is tokenistic at best.*
>
> *The Board and Executive release the strategy for the company, but we never look at it again as a team to see if what we do aligns.*

Compared to comments from people with real input into a collective strategy through a process of engaging and collaborative discussions:

This is the first time I have had the opportunity for active contribution.

We had really great robust debate in the process, and I now see where we need to go.

Seeing the current context of the world outside and how it affects us has made me open up my eyes to the challenges of our work.

My team was able to influence some of the big picture thinking.

We can now see how collaborating across teams could make a big difference to how we deliver.

Rockstars or rocks

Extraordinary outcomes can happen when we bring culture and strategy together. We launch forward with alignment and momentum. Without it, we don't move far. Some become rocks wedged in the ground, not growing or moving at all.

Rockstars

Rockstar companies have high-quality culture and high-quality strategy. The teams work collaboratively and with the purpose to achieve the vision. Engagement and motivation is high. Innovation and creativity are nurtured and there is a clear path forward. Leaders see that team input into the direction of the organisation creates better strategy. The voice of the team and individuals is valued.

Glue

Robots

Teams enact what they're told to do without question. There is no connection to the work or to each other. There's no excitement about it. People roll out the work with no inquiry. It's process line work. When a snag is hit or a strategy isn't working, a culture of action and problem solving is not present. Leaders make changes and inform the team what to do. What follows is frustration and disengagement. People see that they have no influence in shifting the direction of the organisation. They put their heads down and get on with it.

Rioters

Rioters are having a grand old time. In the movie *Bad Moms* (don't judge me) the main character works in a hip coffee roasting company. There are people playing table tennis, and that's all they seem to do. The place is permanently in chaos, held together by about three able people. It's all about the culture, and the work doesn't have the nuts and bolts frameworks behind it. It's probably a place to work for a while – people have fun, love working with each other, but have no strategic direction. People are doing whatever they want. Disconnected brilliant bits of work are in evidence, but instead of forward momentum, it's bedlam.

(Don't mistake fun though as meaning there is no work getting done. Hardhat Digital, a technology company in Melbourne, Australia sees the workplace as a place to live and thrive, not just a place of work. Hardhat took out first place in Melbourne Design 100's corporate interior design award. They have not only set up a deliberatively collaborative office design, as well as an indoor half basketball and downball court, but build people skills on understanding how to function and excel in that environment.)

Rocks

When there is no strategy and direction, and no culture of engagement, you've got rocks. No one's doing anything much. You can see rock type thinking in businesses everywhere when you've got your eye on it. Horsham is a country town on the major highway between Adelaide and Melbourne. There are two Asian restaurants situated next door to each other. One has credit card facilities, while the other does not. Horsham has a large amount of travellers and professional people stopping overnight. No surprises that the one with credit card facilities has many more diners. Next time I came along, the same situation existed. *Rock* thinking. They weren't shifting. They were just maintaining the status quo, while their market walked next door. One restaurant was moving forward. One was working on default and flawed thinking. Sitting and not moving, like a rock.

What would you hear at your workplace?

Workers today are smarter and savvier, looking for challenges and support to grow skills and reach potential. Organisations that focus on only the culture or just the strategy miss the possibility that could come out of bringing the two together.

> Letting people who thrive on excellence collaborate on the strategies that get them to the vision will create extraordinary results.

Clue

A way to start

What's our why?

Have a vision day. What are we trying to achieve here? What is our team brand? Who are our clients/customers? What's our purpose for being? Have a conversation about that. If you are a large organisation, have it in every team, every project. Get the middle leaders facilitating the discussions. Bring together the big theme. Have a whole organisational day. Get people excited about what you're trying to create in the future.

Wonder and possibility

Ask them questions about the vision. Be curious. Get out of your office and ask people what's stopping them from achieving the vision? If that's where we want to head for, what is it that's stopping us? Be inquisitive about that. Talk with people one-on-one or in groups about what is needed to move to get that happening. Start having stimulating conversations that say, yes, we want to shift things. Get people asking questions of themselves to say what is it that we could shift? If we all lifted our game by 5%, imagine the impact we would have? What would move us towards our vision a lot quicker? Create a sense of wonder about that. A sense of possibility, not judgement.

Test stuff out!

Have people design mini projects to try new strategies and new approaches out. Start getting little shifts happening. This builds a culture of proactive change in teams. People are thinking strategically about useful changes and working together to solve problems. Have teams ask: how can we look at doing some small changes fast and quickly and see what we get out of them? Let's not make it big. Let's make it the way we work and doable in the day-to-day. By the teams coming up with these actions themselves and evaluating the impact, a collaborative culture starts to emerge.

Remember

It's not just *what* you do, it's *how* you do it. Get people loving why they do it, and they'll love what they do even more. Get people riding the wave with you. If you don't get your people on board, buying into your strategy, your strategy will never happen, and your culture will never thrive.

Culture does not change because we desire to change it. Culture changes when the organisation transforms. The culture reflects the realities of people working together every day.

Frances Hesselbein, 'The Key to Cultural Transformation', *Leader to Leader* (Spring 1999)

It won't happen overnight, but it will happen.

Glue

From rocks to rockstars

A regional hospital five years ago was in dire straits. The Department of Health was a regular visitor to their board meetings, keeping a keen eye on their performance. With a new CEO in place, the Board and new senior executive worked with me to create the strategic plan. The executive team was excited about the possibility of turning the hospital around. Their higher purpose was clear. They wanted to provide the health services the local people deserved. They wanted to create access to health that was the first choice, not the last option. The executive had a huge strength – they were aligned in the belief that they needed to shift culture and strategy together. One would not work without the other. They had hard work to do.

> They knew that without building connection to the purpose and creating stronger teams, they would fail.

Five years on and the CEO invited me to come and see what they'd shifted around culture, and performance. They are now one of the top performing hospitals in their state. Staff morale and engagement is high, and most importantly, clinical care and patient confidence are on track, delivering a higher standard of care.

The symbols of transformation

On my visit, the CEO took me to see a clear symbol of the shifts that had been made. It took the form of a whiteboard in one of the wards. Most hospitals have whiteboards in their wards or units. However, the symbolism was in the contents of the board and the actions surrounding it. On the top was an inspirational vision about their team. The body of the display showed the data tracked. The number of falls and pressure injuries – a huge issue in hospitals, how long the patients had stayed and other relevant performance measures were all visible. Feedback from patients was written up, and challenges experienced during shifts. There was a problem area. People put ideas up there to address the problem noted. Everyone owned the whiteboard. They gathered around it twice a shift. It's a great example of culture and strategy working together.

This type of work shifted their culture. The staff now have ownership of what is to be achieved. Rather than the nursing unit manager or chief executive coming in with a big stick, people own their results. The team owns the goals. They set what they are trying to achieve. They own their purpose. The glue of purpose and collaboration draws them together.

Chapter Summary

Let culture and strategy have a meal together.

Instead of siloing these important elements, grow them together. Giving people a voice gets you rockstars not rocks. Trust your people with co-creating strategy and the results may astound you.

What's next?

When we work together, let's make sure we've got *authentic* collaboration happening. Most organisations have pedestrian ideas of what collaboration is; it's time we turned them into Rolls Royce ideas. We have a dangerous illusion that we are collaborating when all we're doing is cooperating. The question I pose in our next chapter is: are you collaborating or just pretending?

5
The dangerous illusion of collaboration

Collaboration is not cooperation

Collaboration – authentic collaboration – is something much bigger than cooperation. It's creating something together.

A CEO client of mine shifted her approach from telling people what to do to co-creating the with them. They were growing quickly and had some archaic ways of working to shift. As we put in processes to foster collaboration she would laugh, 'Just don't make us get into a circle and sing "Kumbaya" '. Even though it was tongue in cheek, she had previously seen collaboration as weird. I think she imagined people wearing hessian underwear and standing around in a circle, doing group hugs and having a talk fest. To her credit, she stuck with the process of involving people more. Momentum grew as did buy-in and innovation.

> People get scared about collaboration
> because they think:
> A: it's a waste of time
> B: it doesn't go anywhere.

And they are right in many experiences of 'pretend collaboration'. For people who haven't thought about collaboration as a skill, they believe that you must throw all the rules out the window: of interaction, good communication, having direction, having a plan, and assume it's just a 'festival of love'. That scares people off. And I get that. It's natural to fall prey to the illusion that because we're humans, we must be good collaborators. So, we wave the collaboration flag and say, 'Go for it!'

But our collaboration skills have been beaten out of us. Children have them in bucket loads. Give a group of children a major task to do and then stand back. They put us to shame with the way they work together to achieve a goal. Adults, on the other hand, work in so many companies ruled by silos that we've forgotten how to bring out the best in each other. We need to learn how to do it again.

The illusion of cooperation and coordination

We assume when we communicate something, we're collaborating. We assume when we are sharing information, we're collaborating. We are only cooperating. Moving up to authentic collaboration requires a certain mindset and a range of behaviours for it to succeed. It requires a mindset that's smart and strategic, so when we get together as a group, we have a plan of how are we going to collaborate. What is it that we're doing together? What is it we're trying to achieve? What's our purpose, and how do we stay on track?

> **The most damaging phrase in the language is, 'We've always done it this way!'**
>
> Rear Admiral Grace Murray Hopper
> (*Information Week,* March 9, 1987)

Build a sense of urgency for change

Have you noticed that smaller banks are capitalising on our disillusionment with the distant, uncaring behemoth banks that have most of our money? The larger banks know that their disconnection from the customer is not good for business. Siloed, large departments, stuck in the culture of 'the way we do things around here', have created dislocation and a lack of compassion and understanding of what is going on for customers. There is a long way to go to shift this.

Here is the story of a brave and committed customer who helped her bank start to make a shift to a more human approach. Her name is Pam.

In 2009, Pam, a welfare officer in the education system, was a mother in great pain. Her son Tim had died by suicide a few months before. While dealing with the grief of losing her son, she also had to sort out his financial matters.

Clue

Pam had taken care of Tim all his life. He had always struggled with school, work and life. Pam used some of the money she inherited from her mum to buy Tim a house. It meant he had a small mortgage that was within his means. This arrangement gave Tim the best years of his life.

Tim had not left a will. The inevitable phone calls with the bank ensued after Tim's death.

Pam recalls: 'Knowing that Tim had a mortgage and a personal loan, I needed to contact the bank to work out what the situation was. I started about six weeks after he died. They said they needed all the documents about his death. Then I could become administrator of his accounts. I sent through everything they needed to approve me to act. It was all approved. I started trying to work through the banking. I did it on the phone. I couldn't go to the branch because the matters were all managed in their head office.

'I tried hard to have the courage to make those phone calls, to pluck up the courage to ring and speak to this person on the end of the phone that didn't know me, didn't know the situation. Each time I rang, all I would get was, "Oh we don't have copies of the papers that you've sent in. We'll have to get them, and we'll call you back." That would never happen. They would never call me back.

'Every time I rang, I'd have to tell my story, to be told things like, "We can't speak to you. We can only talk to him because it's his account". And I'd say, "Well, he's dead." And they'd say, "Well, I'm sorry. There's nobody else that can act on this account." It went on for some months with all this to-ing and fro-ing.

'Then the bank contacted me and said because you're closing this mortgage early, we're going to charge you a penalty. My argument was this mortgage is closing because of exceptional circumstances; there should be some leeway here.

'And then there was the personal loan. I got onto a department that handles the personal loans. I wanted to know if there was more than one personal loan and what was the balance. I wanted to pay it out. They wouldn't talk to me because I wasn't Tim!'

'Sorry – our manager doesn't talk to customers'

'I rang the Home Loans Department, which was in another state, and said I wanted to speak to the manager of home loans for the bank. "Oh no, you can't speak to the manager because managers don't speak to customers," they told me. And I said, "Well, I have a problem, and need to talk to the manager." "Oh no, I'm sorry, you can't speak to the manager." I asked, "Well, could you ask the manager for me if I can talk to him?" "Yes." The guy went away, and when he came back and he said, "No, the manager said that they don't have time to talk to you and you can tell me what your situation is." I told him the situation, and he said, "I don't know what to do about this," and he'll get back to me. Well, he never got back.

No one wanted to know. They just wanted this huge sum of money from me but didn't care what the circumstances were.

'And then came a day when I got a girl who seemed compassionate and understanding. I explained the situation, and she listened intently. Then she said, "I'll call you back tomorrow." And I said, "Everybody says they'll call me back tomorrow, but nobody ever does." And she said, "Oh, don't worry. I'll definitely call you tomorrow. I promise I'll call you tomorrow with the answer to this issue." Tomorrow came, and she didn't call back. I felt so let down again. I rang the next day and got on to her and said, "You were going to call me back yesterday, and you didn't." And she said, "Oh yeah, sorry, I forgot."

'I didn't have much fight in me. I was so traumatised. I could only ring in when I had the strength. It took a lot of guts to ring. It was like opening the wound every time, and it was a wound that people were not compassionate about or supportive. I felt like I was thrown to the wolves every time I rang. I felt they couldn't care less. When they knew it was suicide, that again made it another obstacle in the whole picture. Because they didn't want to hear from anybody who had anything to do with suicide. That's all too scary. We'll just get this woman off the phone. That's what I felt.'

Getting up and hitting back at status quo

For Pam, the statement of 'Managers don't talk with customers' triggered off in her a tremendous sense of unfairness and injustice that gave her the strength to keep on fighting.

She sat down and wrote a letter. She outlined every time she had rung in and the response she had received. She wrote about how unsupported and bullied she had felt from these reactions, how rude some of the interactions had been. She wrote from the heart about the difficulties she had experienced. The letter went to the Heads of the two central departments Pam had been dealing with.

She did not receive a single response.

Dejected and traumatised, yet fired up, Pam worked out what the email of the CEO of the bank would be and sent an email outlining her problem, attaching the letter she had previously sent. Within ten minutes Pam's phone rang. It was the National Head of Public

Relations who assured her she would never have an issue with the bank again, as he would personally make sure what she needed was provided.

Pam's long challenge with the bank was over. The financial tangles were ironed out, and Pam could focus on getting on with the other things in her life that had taken a back seat. The senior leader she was working with did everything in his power to make it right.

Creating a sense of urgency for wide-spread change

Back within the bank, they were taking a good, long hard look at themselves. At the highest level, rather than seeing this as an unfortunate blip, this was considered a watershed moment for the whole corporation. I can't say for sure, but I am confident that some of the people involved in the journey of fob offs, lack of compassion and downright rudeness did not stay long in their jobs at that bank. Later that year, at large Manager conferences around Australia within the bank, a session was held where it began with an audio of Pam speaking about her experience. A quietly spoken woman, the pain and trauma of what had happened to her both in her life and through her dealings with the bank were obvious and profound. The groundswell that this had on the people in that conference led to significant changes in the processes that the bank used when it dealt with people suffering from trauma or some difficulty in their life.

A five-step plan was devised showing how they were going to deal with people in general. A way that had more compassion built in became part of the way that bank worked, with Pam's recording used as a catalyst within departments for change.

At the last of the state conferences, the Head of Public Relations introduced Pam herself. 'This whole thing, the reason behind doing

Glue

it for me, was to make a difference. It had happened to me. It wasn't going to make any difference to me what they did next, but it was going to make a difference for the next person. It did. At that conference, after I'd spoken, everybody in that auditorium stood up. It was very emotional for them, as well as for me.'

Pam is one of the most caring and determined people I know. As a welfare officer, she has made the lives of disadvantaged people so much better through her work with them in finding a pathway through whatever system they need to navigate – be it justice, human services, immigration. In her personal life, she has had some of the toughest things happen to her that a person can bear, but she shook up a giant. The day, when at her most vulnerable, someone said to her 'Managers don't talk to customers' created a change that has impacted hundreds of thousands of people.

What was it that was keeping that bank stuck? How could such a situation have manifested? I'm sure all my readers could rattle off many reasons why:

- lack of listening
- lack of empathy and compassion for the customer
- lack of collaboration between departments – systems and behaviours
- avoidance of dealing with stressful situations
- safety in the distance: the further up the chain, the further from the client
- actions not aligned with espoused values
- no organisation-wide approach
- no challenging of the 'way we do it around here'
- arrogance.

We need to get serious. If we don't get together and think about how to shake these up and challenge each other, then either extinction or extreme situations like Pam's are the result. Let's step into collaborative challenge. It's above being nice to each other, cooperating and being harmonious. It's how we push the envelope, and start looking at things through different lenses rather than staying in the comfort zone.

What would be your 'Managers don't talk to customers' moment? How could you get ahead of it by smashing some silos, working together and seeing the world through your customer's eyes?

Start collaborating – really!

Here are some steps to help you shift from coexistence and cooperating to collaborating.

1. Build a collaboration mindset.
2. Identify the levels of collaboration that you need.
3. Build mutually beneficial partnerships and multi-disciplinary teams.

Build a collaboration mindset

I was a business manager in a fine-dining Asian restaurant for several years. In Asian cuisine, one of the foundational dishes is a master stock. A master stock is made from a combination of a whole lot of spices and sauces and rich flavours come together. Within it is chilli, star anise, cinnamon bark, dried mandarin, soy, stock and other fragrant ingredients. The idea of the master stock is it's a

Glue

big, bubbling, flavoursome sauce. The protein, beef, pork or chicken is then put in. It gets poached in this wonderful sauce. A chef's reputation often lies on the quality of their master stock.

A high-quality master stock has got a great balance of hot, salty, sweet, and sour, which is the secret to many Asian dishes. Every day, out of the cool room, the chefs would bring the big pot of master stock for the meats, the big pot of master stock for the poultry. It would be heated up, and then the chefs would add more to it to get the right taste and combination. At the end of the day, after they'd used it, they would boil off all the impurities, and put it back in the cool room to bring it to the correct temperature for storage. In the restaurant that I worked in, the master stock was 17 years old. It started when the restaurant opened. Chefs who are artisans of the Asian master stock say it has got a life to it, a living thing, and you need to treat it with care.

I believe that a collaborative mindset in an organisation is like crafting a master stock. We need to have all the elements: the sweet, the salty, the hot, the sour.

> All these create a healthy, robust challenge. We avoid groupthink. We need a mindset that taps into the diversity that you need to have real collaboration.

Tracey Ezard

contrarian thinking
risk taking
salty
neutralising
outside the box
challenging

passionate debate
spicy thinking
hot
lit with purpose
action

Masterstock

symmetry
aligning
harmonious
sweet
agreement
compelling
valuing

lateral
asymmetry
opposing
deliberating
sour
challenging assumptions

Glue

Don't just go for the sweet

Too often we go on the wrong track with teams. We just want harmony and alignment and agreement and people valuing each other. That is, of course, a critical element. It's the bedrock of the trust that we need to be able to do extraordinary work. But just sweetness will give you status quo. No one open any cans of worms thanks! We like it in our bubble of artificial harmony.

Hot

If we don't have a bit of spiciness, a bit of passionate debate, if we're not linked to purpose, if we don't get action oriented and a bit fired up, then apathy reigns.

Salty

We need people in our teams that give us good contrarian, salty thinking. It makes us look up and challenge our thinking. We get out of the box ideas and risk taking. Without salt we move towards blandness.

Sour

At the same time, we need a bit of sourness in the mix. That edge that says we must do something about this. It's a dissatisfaction with the status quo. This sour approach lifts us out of symmetrical, linear thinking. We open to some asymmetrical approaches, not always looking at things that fit neatly. What do we need to look at that's different, causes dissonance and opposes the symmetry that we might like and be drawn to? How do we spend time deliberating on what could go wrong, and be okay with that sort of thinking? How do we challenge our assumptions? Being ok with NOT agreeing and testing our thinking is critical to high-quality thinking. Too often people with this innate ability are seen as troublemakers. They have a valuable skill – tap into it.

When we mix this thinking and approach, we start to push our status quo, and in a way that brings about exciting change – not anarchy or mutiny – to a vibrant master stock.

Collaboration mindset traps

Our collaborative master stock requires constant attention. Behaviour patterns and mindsets can send it out of balance. To get to that collaborator space of the master stock, be aware of the traps we can fall into.

The Enlightener

Jenny, Sam and Dianne were in the middle of a wonderful meeting. They were designing their approach to the new initiative being rolled out company wide. Good natured banter and non-judgemental linking of ideas helped their creativity. These ideas were fleshed out as they tossed a plan around. Tanya walked in late, sat down and was silent until there was a gap in the discussion. 'I know what we have to do,' she proclaimed and then proceeded to give her dissertation on the process they needed to undertake. Tanya failed to ask a single question about the discussion the others were in the middle of. In her mind, her job was complete. She had enlightened everyone in the room, who apparently didn't know the answer, to the one true way!

Glue

Tanya had fallen into the trap of knowing it all. These are the Enlighteners. They come as the font of knowledge, the person with all the answers. The Enlighteners see that they are there to save the day. Riding in on their white horse, they give the 'correct' answer or approach. They then sit back in the chair satisfied they have rescued the whole project or initiative. People stuck in this way shut down collaboration. The large amount of knowledge, experience, solid ideas and energy that they bring are an asset, of course. But in a collaborative space, everyone's back gets up if the Enlightener is our primary approach.

It also means the Enlightener doesn't grow and learn. They're not willing to throw themselves in and create something more than they had. They're missing what collaboration is all about – that we end up with something better between us than we had by ourselves. Enlighteners don't want their ideas expanded upon. They see it as, 'This is our answer, let's go with it'.

The Lump

The other mindset trap to be aware of are people who choose not to bring anything into the room. These people don't bring their skills or their knowledge. They don't contribute anything, or take anything away. They won't speak up. I call these people the Lumps. It seems a bit harsh, but it occurs because people choose not to contribute. The laptop lid stays up, or the tablet used to reply to emails rather than be present. They choose to not play with others.

The Wasted Space

The Wasted Space is when people are shut down by the processes and behaviours in the room. They have no voice. There may be a few Enlighteners in the room who fill up the rest of the space and leave no room for anyone else. Or perhaps they are new to the team or project, and there is no welcoming environment for them. Maybe they have no idea why they are there; they have just been told to attend. Or, in my experiences with bureaucratic organisations, the rest of the room don't believe they have a high enough classification to add any value (that really gets my hackles up!) and *certainly* not high enough to be a decision maker. What a huge waste of potential. Again, the grinding old paradigm of hierarchy slows us down.

The Vacuum

The last trap that we can suffer from is the Vacuum. We hoover up and take away everyone else's good ideas. We vacuum everything up to take back to our desk, office or team. 'That's great, can you send me that template?' 'Oh, what a great idea, I might go and do that with my own team.' 'Fantastic, who was that person you talked to? Can you send me their details?' This sharing of resources, information and ideas is, of course, a major part of collaboration, but with the Vacuum there is no reciprocation. Their thoughts, approach or intel are not shared in the collaborative space. Things soon wear thin. Generally, people will support others in this development, self-learning phase for quite a while, but goodwill withers when it is simply a continual mindset of 'What's in this for me?'

These mindset traps are dangerous for collaboration. They bounce off each other and create a human dynamic that shuts down creativity and innovation. It keeps us very low on collaboration quality. It maintains shallow collaboration. It becomes about sharing information or telling people what they need to do, rather than co-creating something extraordinary. Creating the master stock dynamic in the master stock is a mindful exercise.

Glue

Ask the questions

To be mindful of these traps, personal self-awareness and reflection of the impact we might have on the group is critical. Group reflection on how we are collaborating is the second step. Ron Heifetz and Marty Linsky, Harvard professors and authors of *Leadership on the Line, Staying Alive Through the Dangers of Leading*, 2002, have a metaphor I love called the balcony and dance floor. It refers to getting people up on the balcony reflecting strategically on what is happening down on the dance floor of their work. We can get so caught up in our dance floor that our heads stay down looking only at our dance floor. We miss vital information and insights.

From the balcony, we can do objective reflection and analysis:

What are our collaborative dance moves?

Do we create an environment where we've got a rocking track on, and everyone is jiving?

Is there good, robust challenge, great thinking, out-of-the-box ideas, and collaboration happening? Or are we shutting down the movement?

Have we got the right music on the dance floor?

Have we got the right steps?

What's my personal impact on the dance floor?

Am I doing the nut bush, while everyone else is doing the sprinkler?

Everyone has a song that gets them on the dance floor

Do you have a song that gets you on the dance floor having a good time? As a former conductor of orchestras and choirs, I would always make sure we had a set of music that would have people either dancing, singing, or moving in their seats. In some situations, we would try for tears of joy. Music is the language of connection. Some songs are simply too irresistible for most people to ignore. With collaboration, everyone has a song that gets them on the dance floor. This is what we could aim for when we are creating our collaborative environment. What beats, rhythms, instrumentation does it have to be successful for us, at this moment, for this initiative/team/project.

> Just like leadership needs to have flexibility to be effective, so do our environments.

One size does not fit all. Different teams or projects will thrive on different beats and songs to work well. When teams ask themselves, 'What is going to work for us?' and set about doing those things, then people are more committed to making it work. Articulate what you all need to make it work, and mindfully go about co-creating it.

Glue

From corrosion to collective capacity

This continuum can be used to identify where are we presenting with various collaborations, and where do we need to be?

Collaboration Continuum

- Collective Capacity — EVOLVE
- Co-creation — DESIGN
- Cooperation — PRODUCE
- Coordination — MAINTAIN
- Co-existence — MAINTAIN
- Corrosion — DESTROY

DISTRUST ———————————— HIGH TRUST

At the bottom, when we have leaders and teams that are actively sabotaging collaboration, corrosion is going on. We are destroying what we're doing. People invested in keeping the status quo use ego and power plays to get their way. Decisions are made that are not for the collective purpose, but for hidden agendas.

Moving up, we find teams and workers who only co-exist. People may have the same title, or be in a work group together, but don't interact at all. They don't share resources or discuss the work. It is the home of the workplace discussed in Chapter Two – silent, siloed and sad.

Many organisations do well at the cooperation and coordination levels. They are mindful of others; they work in harmony. Workload and resources are shared. Tasks allocation ensures everyone is contributing. But they're not designing new things. They keep producing the same products, services and outcomes. It's a maintaining, repetitive space with little forward momentum.

When we shift up to co-creation, we're focused on working as a team, looking at how to do what we do better, and how to co-create together. It's designing; it's ideation; it's trialing things. That is where authentic collaboration kicks in. That's where 21st-Century Tribes come into their mojo. It's NOT about sitting around knitting together and taking up precious time doing little. It focusses us on the work that needs doing. We design and evolve our working and our ways of thinking.

At the very top of the Collaboration Continuum model is the pinnacle of collaboration. One of our primary roles at this level is to build each other's capacity. It's the space of the tribe building the tribe. We build collective efficacy, rather than individual impact. We learn deeply together to increase our collective impact.

Glue

Are you where you want to be?

Recently I worked with a higher education institution focusing on how to support inclusion and diversity in their student cohorts and improve their success. The institution had some programs working throughout the university, chipping away at this goal. Everyone worked hard on their individual program. Great things were occurring in pockets. When the key people and stakeholders spent time using the Collaborative Continuum as a model for discussion, they realised what was happening. There was work going on within the projects, but they were disconnected and working in silos. They needed to make a collective impact, but had no systems connecting them. They had little interaction and no linking communication. There was little or no evaluation of impact.

I call that 'siloed collaboration'. Everyone committed to the one purpose. Within the teams, every project was collaborating within the team. Collective impact needs a whole of organisation approach though. There also wasn't buy-in at the highest level embedding it into relevant plans and policies. They had influential players such as marketing being difficult, as they didn't see the importance of it, and it didn't fit with their vision. They wouldn't play ball.

The group identified many strategies to increase the impact of the whole program through the identification of what was missing and what would enable them to move up the continuum from coexistence to authentic collaboration. They need to do more co-creation and collective capacity building.

What was missing?

With the best intentions, the institution had launched programs to support inclusion but had not articulated a strong vision and purpose. Buy-in from critical decision makers and influencers was not strong enough. Previously, the right people had not been in the room co-creating momentum. People did not have an opportunity to learn from each other. There was no organisational-wide approach.

> Using this Continuum helped the group realise that for collective impact they needed to be up at top of the model.

The university needed to evolve the way they worked with students from a diverse range of backgrounds. They wanted to build an organisation-wide capability to support these groups and have more of those groups succeed and graduate. Instead, the programs were bobbing along at co-existence and cooperation. This was maintaining the status quo and producing pockets of success.

I encourage you to use the Continuum to identify where you are, and where you want to go. Then, what strategies need to be in place to get you there? Key strategies then move these strategies from ideas to action.

Glue

Are you ready to co-create?

The challenge is we rarely move to co-creation. We might get together and discuss our thoughts, but creating something new that breaks down established barriers is a rarity unless we are purposeful. When is it that we need to ideate together to create new ways of working? How can we develop informal and formal means of working together? How can we communicate better? The only people that can answer that is those involved. There are no magic answers – but you can co-create them yourselves if you ask the right questions.

Building multi-disciplinary teams

A multi-disciplinary team is a term that comes from the health sector. The danger of one discipline, such as nursing, or social work, or medicine working with a patient, and not being connected to others can be a recipe for disaster. Unfortunately, this approach to care is a default one still present in many instances. Many experiences in health see patients telling their details and story multiple times. Vital information is not based on in time and incorrect decisions are made about care.

A multi-disciplinary team approach seeks to deal with disconnected and less-than-effective care by getting these disciplines to work together. It means voices, including the patients, are able to contribute. They contribute not only to the diagnosis but also the plan to get the patient well again. Organisations from other sectors are also moving to this sort of approach. Matrix systems that pull expertise into teams for short periods of time are examples of this. Strong project work comes from having a range of disciplines and competences sitting around the 'table', or in the cloud virtually working together.

Our expertise can give us arrogance

Like a warning on the label of a bottle of pills, I have to tell you: authentic collaboration is not easy to do. The journey for the health sector has been bumpy due to hierarchical nature of health that says doctors have the right answer to everything. The power of the position limits collaboration. Changed behaviours from the medical profession in these teams encourage input. For many multi-disciplinary teams this can still get in the way. Nurses and allied health workers such as social workers often feel like they don't have a voice, and that their opinions do not have the weighting that a medical opinion does. There is an entrenched hierarchy that needs major belief change in place. A very senior leader I was discussing this with recently recounted times when she was a play therapist in a hospital setting and being right at the bottom of the 'pecking order'. This is the antithesis of collaboration and multi-disciplinary teams. The ones that are thriving drop the ego and the drive to be right all the time.

> Our expertise can close us down to authentic collaboration.

We can erroneously believe that our training, skill and experience in a particular area give us more right than others to voice our opinions. There is no doubt that drawing from all these things is crucial to making the best decisions. However, the *process* of collaboration needs us to be open to influence and different thinking. If we don't, the mindset trap of the Enlightener is at work. We see our opinions as *right*, therefore making everyone else *wrong*. Time to shut up and listen to others more as soon as we feel this taking over our responses.

Glue

Building beneficial partnerships

Have we got all the right elements that we need, the right skills, the right knowledge, and the right expertise? Who can we partner with to get the outcomes we are seeking?

For GlaxoSmithKline (GSK), one of the largest pharmaceutical companies in the world, collaboration and partnerships are a fundamental pillar of their business strategy. So, when the Melbourne site of GSK wanted to develop new products and a deeper understanding of its processes, it looked for a partner.

> The journey for the health sector has been bumpy and the results that they achieved exceeded their expectations.

Working with Monash University, GKS created the Australian Pharmaceutical Centre of Innovation. As part of this collaboration each year, several students from the university's engineering and pharmaceutical science department collaborate on problems that GSK scientists are trying to solve. The researchers pose a question and work with these students to explore solutions, drawing on the resources of the wider faculty.

The centre started with several projects. They solved some investigations quickly; others evolved into to long-term developments. During the past six years, over 100 students have worked in the centre. For Philip Leslie, Site Technical Lead at GSK in Boronia, Melbourne, involving the students was a big win. 'We have had some great eye-opening outcomes, and results we would have never got if we hadn't had that collaboration.

'For example, one project we worked with the research and development (R&D) team in the United Kingdom on an improved antibiotic formulation. The antibiotic comes as a granule and the pharmacist puts it in water in and shakes it up to dissolve it. The patient then takes it on a regular basis. But the shelf life is quite short when mixed with the water, and it should be refrigerated.

'Our question to the students was: What about emerging countries? First, they don't always have clean water to dilute the antibiotic. And then, of course, they may not have a fridge to store it. We challenged the team to make a stable antibiotic that doesn't need water. They came up with all sorts of formulations based on different types of oils and flavours. We had some great innovation ideas.'

The centre sent these ideas back to GSK's central R&D team, who were working with the charity, Save the Children Foundation, on antibiotics for emerging countries.

For all those involved in the collaboration – the scientists and the students – there is a real buzz to see the practical application of the science they learn in their degree, and to see how they can work in an industry and make a difference. While working with the students, the team at GSK are in learning mode and expose themselves to thinking that is not limited by their daily work and environment. Everyone walks away with more than they started with – whether it be a final product or a new way of approaching a problem.

This powerful collaboration between industry and academia resulted in a new $7.7 million vaccine facility opening at the Boronia site in 2015. The innovative technology used in this new building looks to curb vaccination costs for potentially life-threatening diseases – set off by an initial idea posed in the collaboration.

Glue

Work out upfront what it is you're trying to achieve. Do you already have the skills and abilities that will bring you great thinking, insight and actions? Where do you need to bring others in to be able to fulfil the needs that you have, be it as part of the team, or in the context of a strong collaborative partnership?

In all the strategy work I do in organisations in whatever sector, collaboration and partnerships are a major focus. The determinant as to whether a partnership or collaboration is working well? How strong is the glue – the higher purpose, the connection and the level of trust? When the glue is activated, it doesn't matter what the difficulty is in the mechanics of the partnership; they can be addressed.

Tracey Ezard

Chapter Summary

People work together better when they share ideas.

Co-create, don't just cooperate. No one of us is as smart as all of us. We'll get further together. Purposeful collaboration will reap great rewards.

Buzzing levels of collaboration, with the mindsets that take advantage of the diversity within teams, and between teams can do extraordinary things. We are mindfully creating the environment that allows for interaction and co-creation to occur. We end up new and improved ways of working, rather than the default, 'this is the way I've always done it' type of thinking. And it's exciting and fun too. Some unpredictability to shake things up and have the place buzzing.

What's next?

The very top of collaboration – collective capacity – is a tricky place to reach. It's the pinnacle of a hard mountain. It is about being ok with ambiguity, not knowing what the outcome will be, and co-creating something that wasn't there before. It's also about stepping into an honest and open environment that develops everyone's capacity as part of the group. To be able to do that, we are in the space of learning, and that's what collaboration is all about. Collaboration is learning out loud.

6

Collaborative inquiry and deeper learning

It's been a long week for Danni. She's good at her job, but she is finding it more challenging than usual to get results. Her current project is pushing her skills and thinking so far that she is worried. She's tried all the strategies she has employed in the past, without the results. Not only that, she is aware that her colleagues are watching her struggle. A few of them, who are doing similar work, are also experiencing varying degrees of success. Although Danni's been to a workshop on this subject matter she is finding difficult, when she tried some of the approaches she learned, they didn't work.

Sitting at her desk, Danni realises she needs to talk through her problems. But that isn't the way her team works. You just get on with your job. In meetings, everyone keeps each other up to date with status reports.

In desperation, Danni voices her concerns to a colleague. To her surprise, she finds her teammate is compassionate and confides that he sees parallels between his work and Danni's struggles. Her co-worker also attended the training workshop. The two go back over their reflections on the learning and reach a deeper level of understanding. These insights give both team members more ideas about how to apply the training to the problems they face.

Glue

Back at her desk Danni feels refreshed and invigorated. Talking is such a relief. It stops her problems going around in her head and teases out her thinking in a way that she cannot do sitting at her desk. Her colleague shoots her an email thanking her for the time spent together. Because of their discussion, he writes, he now has some new approaches to problems that had been stumping him. Can they get together again, he asks?

The co-workers begin to spend focused time with each other. Together, they share the strategies they have tried to get projects done. By bouncing off each other's ideas and insights, each finds more useful ways to approach their work.

Collaborative inquiry

Danni has discovered what I call a 'collaborative learning space'. This is a space that people create when they want to increase their understanding, strategies, thinking, and perspectives with others. This learning space enriches everyone involved in it. It works when everyone engages in curiosity and discovery rather than 'tell interactions' or reports. A tell interaction goes like this: 'Tell me your problems, and I'll tell you the solution'. But in the collaborative learning space, we use inquiry. We are never the teacher; we are a contributing participant in a process where everyone is learning. That only happens when we are open to learning. Danni became so frustrated with her thinking that she chose to be vulnerable and open with her colleague. She stepped into learning.

21st-Century Tribes design and create a learning environment within their team. They want a process of collaborative inquiry. They work out what kind of environment encourages a focus on growth for all the members of the team, as well as the role that the team serves in the business. I am not talking about an increase in size; I mean developing and growing quality skills, innovation and creativity.

In my experience, this is not the set up for most companies. Organisations struggle to be in learning mode. Instead, their default is to handball everything to do with 'learning' to the learning and professional development team within the human resource function. That fits with an old, siloed approach to work – each of us work in our own silo of expertise. Leaders sometimes talk about skills development with individuals when it is 'performance plan' time, in isolation from the team. I understand this default. After all, it is easier to stay in this comfort zone than to create a team culture that is built on learning from each other. For decades, leaders have participated in leadership programs that do not even mention how to facilitate a learning environment in a team.

We have a fear of failure. That manifests when our culture focuses only on outcomes such as performance measures. Success and achievement become the only markers of recognition. We create a facade of invulnerability. We become afraid that if we expose areas that need development, we will be cast in an 'incompetent' light. Fear rules the day: fear of judgement, failure, and being wrong.

Deep learning

If we want extraordinary work to happen, we need exceptional team learning. For businesses that want to remain competitive, improvement is the key. To improve, we need a learning environment. What does a learning environment look like? It encourages us to be okay with making mistakes so that we can find new ways of working.

Glue

When we make our projects and our daily work the centre of our learning, our workplace becomes a place of collaborative inquiry. It creates an action-research approach to our business. We continually push ourselves into the learning zone. Rather than our knowledge being disconnected from our work, it is embedded.

Learning is a social activity. When we learn with others, our minds open to other possibilities. Although we think that to admit failure is to be known as a failure, failing and mistakes are a critical part of deep learning. Most organisations do not see mistakes as opportunities; instead, they are problems to be dealt with quickly and quietly. People hide mistakes or ignore them until they become huge, festering problems. We've created a massive belief that being wrong or mucking up is bad.

> For us to be deep learners, we exchange being right for being curious.

We are comfortable with vulnerability, and not knowing. We create an environment where failure is okay. It builds our ability to do unfamiliar things and think in fresh ways. A 21st-Century Tribe creates this environment of learning together. When we understand how to dive deeply into learning as part of the way we work, it becomes a strategic focus of our daily interactions, rather than an afterthought.

Approaches to learning

The difference between current team learning and 21st-Century Tribes is stark. This capability is the defining step to high performance. The chart opposite compares these differences.

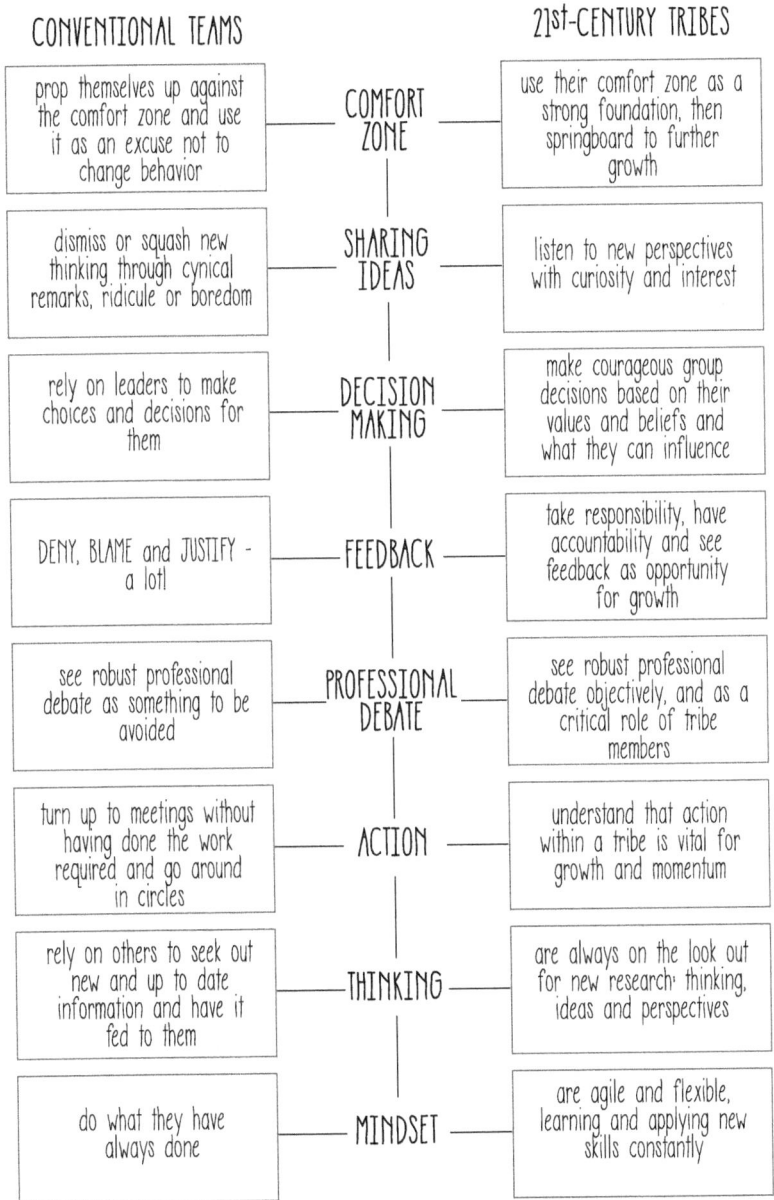

Clue

The open-to-learning mindset: Shoshin

The Zen Buddhist term *Shoshin* means that we are open to learning and see ourselves as beginners. Our mind is empty of preconceptions, and we are willing to consider all pieces of information like we are discovering them for the first time. Dropping our assumptions, we approach learning with the eagerness of a child playing outside. Wouldn't it be fabulous for teams to face up to their trickiest challenges with this sort of attitude? Imagine what we can uncover if we go into conversations to learn a new approach or deal with a problem using this type of playful thinking.

Watch out for these learning traps

The Expert

As we develop knowledge and expertise in an area, our mind can become closed. When we believe we know how to do something, we are less open to other ways of working and thinking. Our expertise shuts down our learning.

When someone without our expertise puts forward a new way of thinking, it tests our open-to-learning mindset. We can block the information or invalidate it. The little voice in our head questions their expertise, qualifications, age or experience. We think, 'How can they come up with a suggestion for me in this arena? I am the expert here!' That is a danger that comes with expertise: we look for information that confirms what we already think. We fool ourselves that we are in a learning conversation, but we are seeking information that confirms our bias. We cherry-pick information that confirms our ideas, instead of watching out for novel ways to approach our behaviours and beliefs.

When we are closed to learning, we don't want to find new ways of working; we only want to validate what we already do.

The Imposter

If we don't believe we have the skills, knowledge or expertise to contribute to team learning conversations, we shut down our thinking and go on 'cruise control'. We diminish ourselves, 'I'm just the administration officer or the marketing junior'. Doing that lowers the group's potential for more evolved thinking and learning. We stop ourselves reaching our full capacity.

A 21st-Century Tribe member is different; she steps into the learning environment believing she has just as much to give as to learn. In her book *Mindset: How You Can Fulfil Your Potential*, 2006 author Carol Dweck discusses the power of our minds. She writes that a growth mindset – a belief that we can grow and develop – changes our ability to reach our potential. A fixed mindset – a belief that we cannot modify the way we think – keeps us small.

Dweck, who is a professor of psychology at Stanford University, shows that people with fixed mindsets see intelligence as static. Success is about talent, not learning. If we stay stuck in a fixed mindset, we have a strong need to look smart.

> When we need to look smart, we feel
> threatened by the success of others,
> rather than being inspired by them.

When people are willing to put themselves into Shoshin, they shift to the growth mindset that Dweck describes. Believing they

Glue

can improve and learn – no matter the stage they are at – they recognise that to learn, they must make some mistakes. They embrace challenges. Their effort is about mastery. Obstacles build determination. When a growth mindset is around, there is a love of learning. It is not about looking smart, but about continuing to push ourselves. In a growth mindset, our colleagues' expertise becomes a well of learning we drink from.

Create a collaborative learning environment

Safety-net strategies

Jogging on the treadmill at my local gym offered me an excellent opportunity to see how we all need different supports to get out of our comfort zones. As I jogged, I looked through the window to the diving pool. Two children about nine years of age tried the middle diving boards for the first time. These boards are 7.5 metres above the water. The first child climbed the ladder. At the base of the ladder, her parents cheered her on and supported her to take the leap. She walked out along the diving board.

If you've ever been on a diving board or even watched them work, you'll know how wobbly they are. The child edged out to the middle of the diving board, turned back around, and went back in. She stood there for a moment watching and then walked back out a little bit further this time. The further she got, the less stable the board, which wobbled up and down. She turned around and went back.

Her dad came up the ladder to the landing with her and stood at her back, quietly talking to her. She walked out to the very end of the diving board, stood still, and looked down at the water. She turned around to her dad and went back to him. Next time, she moved to the concrete platform next to the diving board. It was at the same height, but didn't wobble. Taking a deep breath, she jumped into the water.

The second child went up the ladder, walked out to the end of the diving board, wobbled it a bit to test it out, and then plunged into the water below.

How different we are when we try new things! Some of us need great encouragement and support for certain tasks. We watch other people doing it first. We get people to talk us through it and to let us know that we're going to be safe. For others, we're ready just to go and jump in in the deep end. The same happens with our teams. By building an environment where people can access different supports, we allow them to take a plunge into trying new things and thinking in a variety of ways.

> Feeling comfortable out of our comfort zone sounds like an oxymoron, but when we are uncomfortable, we are in our learning zone.

If we put in place thinking, activities and processes that support us in this learning zone, then we can feel safer to be there. Behaviours that are conducive to safety are needed here as well. Feeling scared to speak up or share our thoughts does not create the environment for learning that an agile and thriving learning tribe needs to blossom. All these strategies are safety nets for taking the risk of being a learner.

Alphabet Inc., the company that owns the global search engine, Google, is known for its determination to push the status quo on how they work. The company set out to study the elements present in their most productive teams. Their two-year project 'Aristotle' uncovered the fundamental concept to be 'psychological safety, a model of teamwork in which members have a shared belief that it is safe to take risks and share a range of ideas without the fear of being humiliated'. Being the algorithm experts they are, they were looking for a list of characteristics common to these teams. Instead, the driving factor was that people felt safe to collaborate on their ideas. Source: 'What Google Learned From Its Quest to Build the Perfect Team', *New York Times Magazine,* February 2016.

Without this safety, the fear chemical cortisol increases in our brain, and our preservation and survival reactions occur before we can consciously stop them. Behaviours such as aggression, shutting down, shutting up, nodding 'yes' but thinking 'no', are all examples of low-safety environments.

There will always be people who are challenged by change and stepping outside the comfort zone. It is scary for some people — for most of us in fact. We have experienced less-than-wonderful behaviour from colleagues in the past, and so we close ourselves off. The safety nets that 21st-Century Tribes put in place are vital. They help us maintain our equilibrium in the learning zone. In a collaborative learning environment, every person in the learning community takes responsibility for contributing to the team safety net.

How can we create the right safety net? Share how you learn best. Discuss what support you need and work to create supports for each person. As 21st-Century Tribes, we bring our individual self-awareness to the table and share what works for us. Then we can put strategies in place that meet everyone's needs.

From toxic to wholesome

I worked with an organisation in serious trouble a while back. It was a toxic environment. People felt scared to speak. An influential clique in the group intimidated the rest of the team. On the Collaboration Continuum discussed in Chapter Five, they were on the bottom rung: corrosion.

Knowing they needed to do something, we arranged to work together off-site to rebuild the bonds between the team and start afresh. Everyone came the night before to have a dinner. Sitting at the head of the long table in the restaurant, I saw the anxiety in some faces. When choosing where to sit on that table, they wanted to be near people they felt safe with. I didn't know any of the participants at that stage, so it was fascinating and sad at the same time to watch them struggle with their fears. During the night, one of the team went home. She was so worried about the next day her fear got the better of her. She suffered what the neuroscientists like to call an 'amygdala hijack', which is when the amygdala in our brain fires off a fear response and triggers one of three responses: fight, flight or freeze. She had taken flight.

For that woman, there were not enough safety nets in place for her to step into the learning zone. The environment of toxicity and tension took its toll. In the middle of the night, she packed her bags and opted out of the effort to repair the damage. She didn't feel able to self-regulate her responses. She didn't trust that she would be safe. What made it even sadder was the fact that the team reached a watershed on the following day. They began to create the 'glue' they needed to bond together as a whole tribe. The process we went through helped them not only to 'see' each other properly without labels, but to co-create the environment they needed to make the change.

Glue

If the learning space is to help us step outside our comfort zone, it must be a compelling place to be. Otherwise, we can go to terror.

Be curious

When someone's interest is piqued, there is greater memory retention, brain researchers studying curiosity have reported in the respected magazine, *Scientific American*. Their article, 'Curiosity Prepares the Brain for Better Learning' (October 2014) reports on fMRI data gained by scanning the brain of research subjects during a range of activities. This shows that when someone is curious, the anticipation of finding out more activates the areas of the brain that make memories and register anticipation and reward. Memory is vital for learning. Anticipation is linked to internal motivation.

**I have no special talents.
I am only passionately curious.**

Albert Einstein

The world would be a better place if we were more curious and less judging. Being curious helps our minds remain active, rather than passive, growing, rather than fixed. Curiosity comes from a position of not knowing it all and from wanting to find out more. It also helps us to be more open-minded. When we are curious, we are open to information and ideas that could change our perceptions, beliefs and approaches to life. There is an excitement in the curious mind. You never know what might come next or which adventure is just around the corner. There is a sense of wonder present among the curious.

> Curious minds are endlessly searching
> for different interpretations of
> the world.

My friend and colleague, Andrew, is full of curiosity. Sitting with a coffee chatting about a whole range of things, I am amazed by his interesting questions. He asks questions to find out what I think at a deep level, rather than at the surface. Quite often I need a long pause to reflect on the question he asked, as I hadn't been curious enough to delve so deep myself.

I am intrigued that Andrew never judges my answer. He is genuinely interested in my view of the world. I try to emulate his skill and ask questions of people just to find out their thoughts, perspectives and ideas – not to pass judgment, or give advice. To be able to do this well, to cultivate an authentic interest in others and the world around is important.

Curiosity is an underrated skill. How often do we sit and test out what it is we believe, what we assume, and what do we think? We've closed down our curiosity. Become a deliberate learning team. Give time for reflections on learning and being curious about the world.

Glue

Drop the need to be right

We're addicted to being right. It's in our DNA, a driving force in our thirst to learn and to achieve success. Our brains give us a rush of a 'feel-good' chemical, dopamine, when we are right. 'See,' our mind shouts out as it provides us with a surge of the chemical. 'I'm right, and it feels GOOD!' If we have an established pattern of receiving this rush, we can also experience intense feelings of frustration and even anger when we don't get it. I've written about this before in my book: *The Buzz: Creating a Thriving & Collaborative Learning Culture*.

The trouble is, when our need to be right overrides everyone else's, we head into territory that is about winning at all costs. That is detrimental on many levels to trust, collaboration and creativity. It kills people's feelings that working with us is worth it – why try to work with someone who always thinks they are right? One or two voices dominate and 'win', and everyone else keeps very, very quiet – it's safer that way. A room full of people with this approach can end up with something akin to a bitter standoff – no one willing to listen to anyone else, and a dangerous feeling enveloping the room. Collaboration demands that we drop our addiction to being right.

> Authentic dialogue dives into the diversity of thought in the room and celebrates it rather than shutting it down.

The more we can self-regulate our need to be right, the more our brain can recode to have different responses. We lose the fears of losing power, looking stupid, or failing, and teach our brain to find other ways to get our 'hit' of feel good chemicals through things such as connection, creating something new, building trust, valuing others, and learning.

It also means that other people in the room feel better. The culture becomes one where opinions count and people are valued. The dialogue based on discovery rather than power. Innovation and creativity are more likely to occur because of the lack of micro-management and control. Most of all – we build a culture of trust – and when we have that, anything is possible.

See failure as opportunity

Teams who mindfully spend time on collaborative inquiry, approach their work with a unique lens to make sure that they keep open to learning. They see failure as a powerful tool for learning. Perfection is not their aim; it's growth. They create an environment of inquiry rather than judgment and stretch the appetite for failure.

For a great insight into how a terrific, innovative company deals with failure and learning in general, look no further than Ed Catmull, President of Pixar Animation and author of *Creativity, Inc: Overcoming the unseen forces that stand in the way of true inspiration*, 2014. At the end of every movie production, rather than move onto the next project, they hold a post mortem. Whether the film was a success or failure, it doesn't matter. This reflection time is just as important as the actual work.

There are five reasons Catmull poses for doing a postmortem:

1. Consolidate what everyone learned.
Allows for learning to be done on the job and reflected upon with more focus and with the benefit of hindsight.

2. Teach others who weren't there.
A seize-the-day opportunity to pass on the learning to others, as well as challenge some thinking that may have gone on.

3. Stop resentment festering.
Take the lid off a simmering pot of ill feeling, misinterpretation or miscommunication. This creates better relationships.

4. Use the schedule to force reflection.
Spend time preparing for the post mortem. Catmull believes that most of the value of the postmortem occurs in this lead-up time.

5. Pay it forward.
Frame the right questions for the next project.

The postmortem ritual at Pixar Animations places failure where it makes the most impact – as a learning opportunity. What are your rituals and symbols around failure? Do they enhance learning or make failure wrong?

The collaborative learning roles

Collaborative learning draws on four roles for success. Every member of the team needs to access them all for the learning culture to be healthy. Becoming adept at these skills provides the environment where we are challenging our thinking and knowledge. Accessing these roles takes the learning process from purely in our heads to a combination of outward inquiry and inward reflection.

At the hub of the Collaborative Learning Wheel is the learner growth mindset we have already discussed. One that has an open to learning, Shoshin approach. In this mindset, we are curious and see failure as opportunity. We understand our learning preferences and what safety nets work best for us. The four other roles form the spokes that set up an environment of deep learning with others:

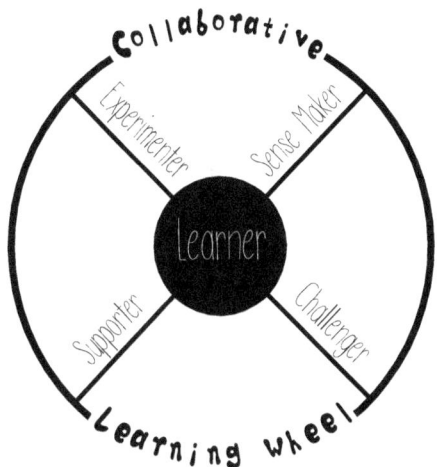

Sense maker

The world is drowning in information. The information and data we have created in the last two years have been more than the history of man. This curve of information overload will only increase in the future. We end up feeling like we are drinking out of the proverbial fire hydrant. When we are in sense maker mode, we take the massive amounts of information, insights, opinions and seek to gain clarity. The Future of Work 2020 report from the Institute of the Future names sense making as its number one skill of the future. The report definition is 'the ability to determine the deeper meaning or significance of what is being expressed'. We open the lens of our thinking beyond our first thoughts and assumptions.

Clue

When we are in the sense-making mode, curiosity is our primary ally. It helps us make sense of the information we have. Asking questions changes our perspective of our work so we see more clearly.

> Where do we want to go?
>
> What would we do differently in this scenario?
>
> How could the change in the policy/ procedure/ team structure impact on this project?
>
> What assumptions have we made?
>
> What do the numbers tell us?

We also think from a strategic perspective about the issue at hand – a balcony view of our dance floor. We sort through the data, the numbers, the insights that we have, and identify the points that are critical.

> What is non-essential?
>
> Is this conversation taking us down a rabbit hole that is not useful for our end game?
>
> Where are our measures of success?

When teams visually make sense of this information, we see things that allow us to learn more about what we're trying to do. Visualisation of data and our thinking helps us to see patterns more quickly. One team I worked with visually tracked the customer's journey. Having it up on a large chart on the wall created a big 'aha' for everyone when the loop they had set up in their processes became apparent. The team stood around the chart and wrote up questions along the journey to provoke their thinking. They drew different versions of the journey. They then set about coming up with a plan.

Experimenter

We never leave status quo if we're not willing to give things a try. Being an experimenter means that we play lightly with our learning. We try things without a huge fear of stuff going wrong. It's the key **DO** element into such methodologies as the PDSA or PDCA approach.

The PDSA **cycle** is shorthand for testing a change in four steps:

1. Develop a **plan** that will test the change (**Plan**).
2. Carry out the test (**Do**).
3. Observe and learn from the impact and consequences (**Study**).
4. Determine what modifications are needed (**Act**).

Here the whole team is firmly in their learning zone. The play lightly approach is necessary – small tweaks of how we work, stand back and see if it does! If not, try something else. If we're going to experiment, what we're looking for is the impact. We're looking for outcomes that will take us toward our goal.

Supporter

Another critical role of being a learner in a collaborative space is to be one of the supporters. If everyone is trying to do things in a different way, we need to stop judging and start supporting others and ourselves to try different things. That way, we are not frightened of criticism of our decisions that keep us doing the same. It's about

Glue

making it comfortable to fail. It's also about just being there when someone is having a tough time, of trying something tough, giving them a bit of 'ra ra' so that they feel okay about the fact that they are in this together.

For Danni, who we met earlier in this chapter, her colleague's compassion for the bind she was in and supportive approach enabled her to stay in a learning space, rather than give up. When people take a risk with each other, there's vulnerability to support. We can make it safe to be vulnerable, or unsafe. Invulnerability is a facade that we put up, which railroads our learning and creates an inauthentic approach to our work.

Challenger

Challenging thinking through robust discussion is essential to great collaboration and creativity. Challenging our reasoning elevates us out of the ordinary. Exploring our beliefs is an important part of a collaborative learning process. Authentic collaboration is learning out loud so articulating our assumptions, and challenging our thinking with each other, moves us to a space of deeper learning.

How to get started

Be prepared to ask for help

Sometimes we don't see that it's our thinking that's keeping us stuck. We worry what we'll look like, that we'll look like we're failing, or unable to do the tricky stuff. In reality, colleagues are more than happy to help. Teasing out thinking as a team can be incredibly liberating, as well as a great bonding exercise. It takes away the subjective, 'You're wrong,' approach and says, 'What if we thought differently? What might this look like? What are the assumptions that we have?'

Be okay with discomfort

Discomfort is a sign of stretch and growth. It's the learning zone where we build our capabilities. Recognising discomfort as a learning opportunity builds self-awareness. It helps us stay out of the blames and justifications when someone is trying to see a new path. Feeling uncomfortable is a great physical reaction that shows that there's learning going on.

Be curious. Practice Shoshin

In a collaborative inquiry space, investigate and explore before coming up with approaches that might work. 'Inquiry' is the critical word here. We want to test our thinking in a safe and objective environment. Take on the Shoshin approach of thinking as if you were beginners at what you do. What if? How could we? What would happen if ... ? Is it possible? What would we find? What thinking could we use here? Learn from each other's experience. Tell me how? What made you try? What was your approach when? What worked best in that situation?

Modelling excellence is another way that we can be curious, and aim for extraordinary learning. Look at the people who are creating success. What are they doing? How could we approach that and try that ourselves? What is that we can learn from them?

Chapter summary

We need to get better at learning together if we want to collaborate.

The tribe that learns together wins the game. With no learning, there is no growth, and discomfort equals growth.

Imagine if your teams were buzzing with the challenge, and supercharged by learning with and from each other? Imagine if the environment was one of lifting each other up to even better heights? Imagine if people didn't shy away from not knowing. If they sat with ambiguity and said, 'I don't know. What do you think?' rather than hanging onto a veneer of being right. What sort of extraordinary work could you do if the learning zone was your preferred place to be?

What's next?

If learning is critical to collaboration, innovation and challenging the status quo, how do we even create the environment where people are willing to take risks, be vulnerable, and show up ready to learn? We need the super glue that will give us the cohesion to create a thriving team learning environment.

We need the glue of trust.

Part III

The Glue of Trust

Compassion

Connection

Conversation

A litte segue before launching into part three.

What's trust got to do with it?

I am fortunate to work with organisations trying hard to find the right recipe for forward momentum. The brake on momentum often comes down to this: people feel a lack of trust. Even if it is the processes not being quite right, the product not meeting customer needs, or the strategy missing the boat, underneath all that, the thing keeping them in a holding pattern is a lack of trust.

Often it's a lack of trust in the leadership. A feeling of 'us' and 'them'; of hidden agendas and a general unsafe feeling; of not wanting to open our mouths in case it gets used against us; of leaders taking the credit for hard work we've done, or great ideas we've had; of seeing leaders sabotage each other to get ahead. Just as frequently, it's also about a lack of trust in each other.

People have great relationships out of the workplace. For some reason, we've set up in our work environment the idea that when we walk into the front door, we behave differently. Without the right environment and connection, we keep a distance from one another. We lose our authenticity. And when we lose our authenticity, we lose trust. People are distrustful of superficial, artificial relationships. But we've become accustomed to that being the way of the world in the workplace. And it's making us more unhappy and demotivated than ever before.

Lack of trust comes down to people putting more time and focus on tasks than relationships. Trust springs from everyone in the team seeing that part of their role is to create bonds with each other; to step out of self and connect with other people that they work with. That is what elevates teams to real tribes.

The title of this book gives a hint of the difficulty in identifying the intangibles of collaboration, connection and learning, and the strength they bring. Glue, when it brings two or more elements together sets into an invisible force. It is hard to see yet its power is felt. Because it is not a *hard* measure, many of our executives don't want to know about it. And yet without that invisible glue, we fall apart. Fortunately, the latest research shows it does impact hard measures. Throughout this book, research points out the effect of these elements on the bottom line, talent retention and innovation. Exciting research into trust contributes to the case for companies to spend time building trust.

The elements of trust

For glue to work, we need two major forces: one is adhesion, and the other one is cohesion. The way water works is a good way to explain these concepts. Cohesion is when molecules connect to like molecules. Think of rain falling from the sky. Cohesion keeps the particles of water together. When they stick together, they form a droplet.

Adhesion is about sticking to another thing – when one type of molecule connects to another that is different. When the droplets hit our window, and the water connects with the glass, adhesion keeps the raindrops stuck on the window. They fall when they become too heavy for the adhesion to hold.

In this last section of the book, we'll be looking at the three critical elements of glue that will give you the adhesion and cohesion you need to create high trust. Trust that will see you through challenging times and fabulous times. We will look at the adhesive of purpose and the bond of cohesive relationships.

The latest research on the brain shows clearly that when we feel trust, chemicals such as dopamine and oxytocin rise in the different regions of our brain. Oxytocin looks to play a big part of social bonding and empathy. When this neurochemistry in the brain is activated, it seems that the prefrontal cortex works far more effectively. The prefrontal cortex is the executive function of the brain. When we're operating in this part of the brain and in this trusting state, we're able to problem-solve, collaborate, have empathy and think rationally. It's where we access our higher-order thinking. When we are in a fear state, we shut down our thinking and move to a survival mode instead.

Therefore, when we trust, we work better. When we are confident, we're able to dig deep into how to solve the problems that are facing us. When we distrust, on the other hand, we retreat from this part of our brain and are driven far more by the limbic brain, the emotional seat of our brain. Threat and fear rise, and we find it far harder to work to our full potential. Trust is a critical element to enable us to fulfil our potential.

Glue

Paul Zak, the founding director of the Center for Neuroeconomics Studies and the author of, *Trust Factor: The science of creating high-performance companies*, 2017, has done a significant amount of research over decades on the difference between low-trust and high-trust companies. He and his colleagues use neuroscience as a base of this investigation. They have some surprising findings, as reported in *Harvard Business Review*, 'The Neuroscience of Trust', January 2017.

Paul Zak's findings show:

74% less stress

14% less burnout

13% less sick days

76% more engagement

29% more satisfaction with their lives

106% more energy

50% higher productivity

in high-trust companies compared to low-trust companies.

This is a game changer for us. Through neuroscience research, we can see that connection between people, and the trust we build between people, is a critical element of success.

What this science helps us to understand is that here lies our focus. It's no longer any use to look solely to strategy, or task to make change. We must focus on how our people connect, both to what they are doing (their day to day tasks) and to each other.

Finding the keys to trust will help new members come into your tribe and become high-performers fast. It will help you connect with your customers and create loyalty, and increase your market. It will create the environment where you become an employer of choice. The best performing staff are looking for workplaces where there is strong trust because purpose and fulfilment are their driving factors.

The glue of trust

These ideas are so important and so central to my work that I created a model to help you visualise trust, understand the components that make it up, and unlock the secret that creates it. There are three elements in the Glue of Trust model: connection, compassion, conversation.

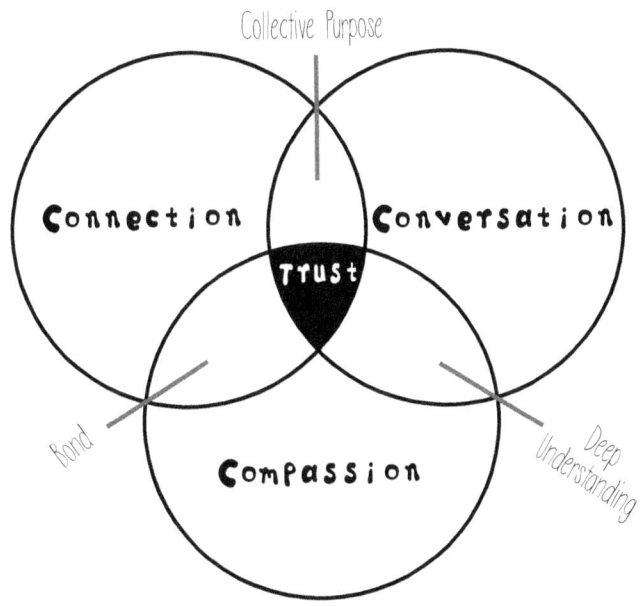

In this section, we will look deeply at each of these elements, starting with connection.

You deserve to work in an environment of trust. And, when you can bring those three elements together, you will have a bond with your team, a thorough understanding of each other and, most importantly, a sense of shared, collective purpose.

That's what builds trust – and that's what builds 21st-Century Tribes.

7 Connection

Connection

I love eating in restaurants. It's one of my favourite pastimes. I enjoy sitting and eating in a place where the wait and kitchen staff and are just as passionate about the food and the service as the owners are. It shows don't you think? The way they welcome you as you enter, the interaction at the table as you look at the menu, the care they take with the delivery of meals. Restaurants with open kitchens always fascinate me. Watching chefs who work incredible hours continually plate up meals that delight the diner is like watching an orchestra at work. In some of the frenetic Asian cuisine places I enjoy most, it's like watching a rock band performing.

One of my good friends, Ben Cooper, is Executive Chef at the Lucas Group. Their 'mothership' restaurant is Chin Chin, one of the most successful and delicious restaurants in Melbourne. I worked with Ben years ago in another restaurant. Even back then he cooked with all this heart and soul. His connection to his higher purpose is so strong that it drives him to create amazing dishes that he is renowned for. He is committed to his staff and helping them deliver food that they are proud of. I talked with Ben about trust and creating successful tribes (something the Lucas Group appears to be highly adept at!) as I was researching this book. I asked him what some of his secrets were to build trust and connection to purpose in his staff. He said that early on in his career as a senior chef, he had been 'tearing strips' off a junior chef who had made a mistake. He stopped short in the middle of it, and it struck him that if food cooked with love is the best food, then food produced with anger is the opposite. This realisation was a major driver to him focusing with love rather than frustration on his staff. With his words and his actions, he was more purposeful about building others up rather than tearing them down. It was aligning his purpose as a chef to his purpose as a leader of his tribe.

When you eat at a restaurant where the food and service are driven by love for what they are creating, it is an experience that brings you back again and again. When you are the recipient of teams who have spent time getting very clear on **WHY** they are there and **HOW** they connect to achieve that – the experience for the customer is one of delight, and of the tribe is one of deep fulfilment.

Connect quickly

In 1965 Bruce Tuckman created what is affectionately known as the 'Orming model'. This model is still used around the world and is a useful lens to see teams through. The model begins with teams coming together and 'forming'. They move through the stages of storming, norming, and performing. Trust builds through a cycle, as do the team norms of behaviour. For some organisations, they stay stuck in storming and never move out of it. I've worked with teams that have been storming for 20 years! Instead of perturbating for a while sorting out dynamics and moving to norming, they are held there by unprofessional behaviour. Behaviour ignored is behaviour condoned, so the team remains stuck. Or teams head back to forming as soon as new people join, and go through the whole process again.

We no longer have the luxury of time to sit in re-forming. Getting people inducted, feeling safe, valued and connected to the purpose and individuals in the team moves them quickly around the cycle. As more flexible team membership becomes the norm, we need high performance to be the default, rather than having to constantly go back to the beginning stages of forming.

Connect to purpose

When we build a strong connection, we increase the engagement of our team. Our team feels that we're working together on achieving the collective purpose, and willing to shift and leave the status quo to get to that higher purpose. We become galvanised around it. We start to see the connection between our work and that purpose. We make conscious decisions based on that end goal.

The main game is to move *together* to this purpose. If people are all heading in different directions, it dilutes the opportunity to get there. Whereas if we bring people together heading in the same direction, the momentum built is far stronger. The chances of getting there become higher and the speed faster.

> Spending time creating and articulating our purpose is time well spent. It forms the glue of trust that engages people with the work.

It helps us to implement meaningful change and find meaningful purpose in our work. When people connect with their hearts, their mind follows. It's no longer enough to tell people what they must do. They need to feel it with their whole body.

Glue

Lack of understanding around purpose can lead to demotivation and emotional detachment, which leads to a disengaged workforce. The Chartered Institute of Personnel and Development, CIPD UK, sharing research in their 2010 report *Shared Purpose – the Golden Thread* found that organisations with a shared purpose outperform those with none. The time we put in here is relevant to the bottom line. It shows up in the perceived 'softer' measures of workforce engagement and morale, but it also impacts on the hard measures of the bottom line as well. The lines of people waiting to get into Chin Chin every day and night are qualitative proof of that.

Connect fast and you will 'future-proof'

Future proofed organisations are more flexible. Flexibility means we can move people so that we tap into the skills particular projects may need. Teams are changing membership more fluidly. Getting people clear on their purpose for being there and who they're working with enables them to build trust as quickly as possible. We haven't got the luxury that we used to of having a long time to build relationships, get to know each other well and construct the norms of the team.

Disengagement is hurting us all

Research shows that disengagement costs us huge amounts of money; it also costs society through unhappiness and disconnection. When people are disengaged and unhappy at work, they carry that back into their private lives. More people show that they're feeling overwhelmed, overworked, and underappreciated in the workplace. This is contributing to a wider source of social isolation and disconnection, clearly linked to an increased burden of disease and ill health. 'Blue Monday' is now a term used to reflect the feeling of dread many people have going back to work after the weekend.

Three into one equals success

Over the last year, I've been working with three small schools in a regional town. Those schools have been going for a long time. In fact, one of them has been going for 150 years. They are all moving to become a new school the following year, amalgamating on a new site with a brand-spanking-new school. At the start of the process, there were three very separate tribes. These tribes had their own ways of working. Even though they are all places of education, the way that they work was entirely different.

There was also a sense for some, of, 'This is our school, and we don't want to become part of another school'. We had the challenge of creating a new tribe.

Before our first day all together, I went around to the three schools, and we did a large journey map of their story. What were the achievements? What were the significant things that had happened to them in their history? What was it that they had learned? What were the things that they were most proud of? What is it that made them uniquely 'them'? We charted it up on big sheets of paper. This process also gave me an opportunity to get to know the three different groups that I'd be working with through the year.

Our first day all together was to do vision and purpose work to set the scene. With many people not knowing each other, it was important that people connected and that we created a sense of the vision of the new school and what purpose did we want as a new tribe. Our day together began with us spending time sharing those stories. The groups broke into smaller teams mixed from the three schools. Everyone went outside under the trees, sat around and shared their stories and asked questions of each other. We did a lot of discussion about trust and the neuroscience of trust. We discussed how we could short circuit the journey to a connected tribe.

Seeing ourselves as part of the tribe

Throughout the day we continued to have conversations about the purpose and the vision of the school. What was it we were trying to create for the students? How did we want to 'be' in our new school? How do we involve our community? That sense of tribe started to occur where people no longer saw themselves simply as from their previous school but as a contributing member of the creation of the new school.

If the people at each school had not committed to spending that time, connecting to their vision and purpose of the new school, and connecting deeply as people, the challenging journey would be much harder.

Connect as a team to the higher purpose of the work

The need for purpose drives human beings. People who turn up to work every day without a clear sense of their purpose feel unfulfilled. As a team, as a tribe, for us to sit down and articulate our mission is a useful activity to undertake. And it needs to be a purpose that is not profit driven.

The reason people go to work is not merely to create dividends for shareholders. It creates great cynicism and disconnect. People are becoming more concerned with the rate of consumerism and the drive to make more money. The Deloitte Millennials Survey 2016 of 7,700 millennials surveyed globally states that almost 9 in 10, 87%, believe that the success of the business should be measured in more than just its financial performance. It also found that those likely to remain the longest share their organisation's value and are more satisfied with its sense of purpose and support of professional development.

Some examples of company purpose:

IAG Insurance: 'We help people manage risk and recover from the hardships of unexpected loss.'

Patagonia outdoor clothing and gear: 'Build the best product, cause no unnecessary harm, use business to inspire and implement solutions to the environmental crisis.'

IKEA: 'To create a better everyday life for people.'

As a team, also have your own purpose. For example, an internal data team's purpose might be: 'Helping our teams make great decisions'. Think about the role the team plays and the impact it has. My suggestion is not to get bogged down in long-winded mission statements that have everyone snoozing before the end of the first paragraph. A short, snappy purpose sentence that sings will do the trick.

Examples of team purpose:

Alcohol tobacco and other drugs therapeutic counselling team: 'Helping people find their voice.'

Hospital food service: 'Providing nutritious and tasty food to help people recover well.'

Business valuation team in a top-tier accounting firm: 'Giving legally and ethically sound advice for our clients' best financial outcome.'

The role of those purpose statements is to inspire us. It's to get our heads up to say, 'We do have an important mission here, so let's not be mediocre about it. Let's not be happy with the status quo if we're not meeting it. Let's work together.' You've got to have a collective, to get collective purpose happening.

Find your why

Simon Sinek became well known through his TED Talk 'Start with Why' as being the guru of purpose. His 18-minute 2009 TED Talk is some of the best minutes a team can use to set their sights on crafting their vision and purpose. It helps us to understand how important the why is for our most primitive brain, the one that seeks a purpose, the one that seeks to understand what's important to us at our very core.

The five whys can be a useful way for a team to find their higher purpose. The five whys are often used in business to drill down into root cause analysis around an issue. I like to use them for teams to lift their eyes up – in the other direction. When you look at the major goal or mission you have a team, ask yourselves: 'Why do we want to reach this goal?' then ask the same question up to five more times until you have an answer that resonates for everyone like a bell. It will become apparent when you have reached and connected to the pinnacle why – and it will help you move forward.

David Sibbet is an American organisation development expert. He has worked for four decades with organisational development using visual tools to create purpose. I learnt from David during a course in Berlin and was introduced to the Drexler/Sibbet Team Performance™ Model, created in collaboration with Allan Drexler. It's a model I use extensively when I'm working with organisations.

Based on the idea of a bouncing ball, it has seven stages to it. The seven steps move through: orientation, trust, goals, commitment, implementation, high performance, and renewal.

> When you spend quality time on the first three stages of the model, the bounce of the ball as you reach commitment is much stronger.

Think of a tennis ball that is soggy and full of water. When you bounce it, it goes splat on the ground. The model reflects the idea that if we don't spend time on the first three stages, orientation around purpose, building trust, and being clear on our goals, then we won't bounce with vigour to commitment and implementation. We can't expect people to commit to work when we haven't done the work setting the purpose, connecting people, and being clear on what we're working on.

Clue

Co-create your team's purpose

As a team, sit down and have the conversation giving a language around your purpose. Connect it to the higher purpose of the organisation. If that organisational purpose is unclear, ask for clarity. Seek to push the company to be clear on what they're trying to achieve and their purpose. Manage up if you feel that the information coming from above is vague. When people don't see, and feel a clear purpose, they feel disengaged and demotivated. When you ask people in a team, 'What's the aim of this team?' There ought to be an exciting and motivating statement to use as a mantra. When we have the right one for our team, it resonates like a bell.

Connect to each other

The people we work with become part of our tribe, but we need to get to know them and see their humanness. I've worked with teams before who have come together in a restructure, and after three months people still don't know someone on the other side of the room. They have not created systems that allow for people to interact and get to know who they are and how they contribute to the whole.

David Rock, a neuroscience expert who runs the NeuroLeadership Institute, and is the author of *Your Brain at Work Strategies for Overcoming Distraction, Regaining Focus, and Working Smarter All Day Long*, 2009, says that 'People you don't know tend to be classified as foe until proven otherwise.'

It's nearly impossible to have any element of trust when we still see each other unconsciously as the enemy. While this seems to be harsh and a bit unreal, neuroscience shows that unless we experience that oxytocin of feeling connected to someone, then we do feel an element of threat.

Understand what people's skills and attributes are and what's important to them

Doing this is an excellent way to go underneath the surface of what we show. Unsafe and untrusting environments make it safer to keep a distance from each other. We put up a façade. Understanding people's motivations is an important element of having an environment where people feel valued.

If we never go near those conversations, we're making assumptions about what is important to people. Perhaps we don't care what's important to people. Thriving tribes *do* care and understand what it is that drives people to do their best.

Connect quickly

Observing how teams respond to new people who show up is a good indicator of how well a team connects quickly. If, as soon as someone joins a team, others roll their eyes at any mention of their previous experience, that's a pretty good indicator that they don't want to understand where this person has come from and the experience and the talent that they could bring into the team. 21st-Century tribes focus on understanding the value each person brings to a team and working out how to increase that value through collaborating and tapping into skills.

In the 70s, sociograms were all the rage in education but also in some organisations. People would map the interactions in a classroom/

team and see who were the social isolates and who were the ones with a lot of connections. If we sat above our teams and looked down at the interactions going on, there would be some people in parts of the team that never get accessed. They never interact. It might be because of geography or systems not put in place to have connections forged, or it might be by choice. If people never intersect meaningfully, we won't get trust happening, and we certainly won't get collaboration happening.

Share something of yourself

Meg was part of a newly formed leadership team. The team wanted to make a major impact on the way their unit ran and be clear on their purpose. While spending a day creating their leadership vision, they shared their journeys. I asked them to draw the pivotal moments in their leadership journey that shaped them into the leader they are today. Two important learnings came out of it. One of them was that Meg was told by one of her first mentors to keep a distance between her team and herself and not to get too close. Meg is a people-person; she had suffered from taking on that advice. Relationship and connection is important to who she is. She wasn't being authentic. It meant that there was a major disconnect and distrust between the team and Meg. In her next leadership role, she flipped that and built strong relationships with her team. She made more progress with her team due to the trust they built through their connection.

On the same leadership team, Jason shared his journey of being a single parent after the death of his wife and how it had shaped his leadership. He spoke of his commitment to 'respectful challenge' to create an innovative environment within the team. His experience of challenging his own assumptions of being a parent led him to challenge the status quo in his work.

As each of the leaders shared their journeys, understanding and compassion connected them. This sharing of personal history only served to deepen the conversation we had that day about how they worked together. When we tell the stories of our past and the stories of things that are important to us we create connection.

Find the joy in the work

Often I ask people to share a moment of joy they experienced with their work in recent times. There's usually a stunned silence when I ask that question, and then people find it. I ask them to think about a time something happened that made them reflect, 'This is why I get up in the morning'. The energy in the room seems to expand during this discussion. Why don't we do that more often? Why is it that we focus so much on the things that are hard, the things that are dragging us down, rather than things that can give us joy? It is the same with fun.

Joy and fun both increase oxytocin. They increase our happiness. Why shouldn't parts of our work life give us pleasure? Neuroscience shows that increased oxytocin gets us working more functionally in the pre-frontal cortex of the brain. This is the part of the brain that does our heavy cognitive lifting.

> If we can increase the amount of joy we have, the better we think, connect, and collaborate.

Clue

Co-create the way you want to work

Several years ago, I was fortunate enough to work with a new organisation connecting their people not only to the purpose of their work but the way that they worked. The whole organisation had a higher purpose statement and values that were inspiring. The Human Resources team had worked closely with the staff to develop them. To support these, we were to set up a leadership capability framework for the whole staff. They were after a structure that was applicable to every staff member, not just the leaders. It was to be co-created by the staff themselves.

Through staff meetings and working together on a voluntary group project, we created the framework of capabilities. They were passionate that it should reflect the important attributes driving every one of them. As the process evolved, it was filtered back through to the whole staff for further input and feedback.

The staff wanted the values of the organisation to guide them. They felt strongly that they should embed in *how* they worked. They were the foundational values of respect and integrity, followed by collaboration, diversity, innovation and responsiveness. These made part of the framework.

They also came up with a set of core capabilities applicable to all members of the organisation, no matter what level. It covered four areas they felt represented the key attributes of people working in the business. It was deliberately written in the first person, rather than the impersonal third person statements often found in similar documents.

Self aware

I use reflective practice to assess my impact
I am aware of my skills and attributes
I am aware of the impact of mood states and body language
I understand what motivates me

Motivated

I am willing to grow and learn
I approach work with a positive attitude
I motivate others around me

Values driven

I understand and articulate the values of the organisation
I am open and transparent
I model and uphold the values of the organisation
I consider the organisation's values in all work practices

Solution oriented

I approach work challenges proactively
I constructively problem solve issues and new ideas
I explore all relevant perspectives and opportunities

Further capabilities were developed under the specific headings of: contribution, stakeholder relationships and engagement, improvement. The capabilities developed under these headings increased in responsibility and skill from *core* (whole staff), through to *lead and manage*, then *inspire and enable*. This last level was for, but not limited to the executive level.

This process was a symbolic act of co-creation and collaboration from everyone in the organisation. Feedback loops ensured that teams fed into the process through their representatives.

Clue

The executive team had one representative who was an active participant, but not the driver. The organisation used the capability framework in recruitment as well as in mentor discussions and one-on-one development discussions. As you can imagine, there was a strong connection between these people to not only their higher purpose but also to the work and the way that they did that work.

'So what?' you may say, we have more capability frameworks than you can poke a stick at. (In fact, when I google those words, instantly I get 92,600,000 hits.) Hey, and wouldn't they be *way* out of style for 21st-Century Tribes?

The difference is – it was theirs, and theirs alone. They wanted it, they created it, they owned it, and they wanted to live it. The words articulated the connection they had to the purpose and the work. The process and the product were important parts. The certainty, agreement and alignment they ended with, through this process, was the pivotal one.

Chapter Summary

Connected people are happy, healthy and engaged.

When we understand the why, the what and the how follows. To trust is to connect and without connection, we wither. When we're striving for the same thing the momentum becomes much stronger and the journey much easier. When we truly connect to each other, there is a strong sense of tribal connection that gives us the cohesion we need to do the hard work.

What's next?

Guess what? We can feel totally in sync with the direction of the team and work, and *still* find relationships tricky to work with. Working with people *is* tricky. Personalities, miscommunication, and fixed mindsets can all upset the apple cart. Just *saying* that we want to build trust between people is not enough. We need to have behaviours that match.

What is the glue needed to create a strong and flexible connection between us? The remaining two chapters will give the final elements of the glue that will help our tribe truly connect to each other through thick and thin.

 Compassion

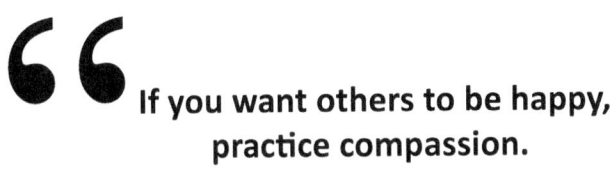

If you want others to be happy, practice compassion.

His Holiness, The Dalai Lama

There is something deeply satisfying when someone 'gets us'. They have listened to what we are feeling without trying to solve anything. We feel heard, and we feel valued. Trust increases. We feel seen rather than judged. Our ability to see the world through someone else's perspective builds compassion for each other.

Compassion helps our tribe feel supported, and our feelings acknowledged. There's so much shutdown that goes on in teams and organisations; people's feelings are invalidated, or not even sought. We keep on hammering at people to try to get them to achieve more, work faster, increase their efficiency. All this without considering how they are feeling and what might be going on for them. We're not getting the best out of each other, and we're not creating the space where we feel supported and nurtured as people.

Glue

Compassion, not empathy?

I work regularly with leaders and teams in the health sector. Working with female doctors and surgeons, we have interesting conversations about how the critical need for compassion for patients. High levels of empathy do not serve you as well as compassion. If you go too much into a full empathetic state with people in distress, it can be very detrimental to your mental wellbeing. One doctor spoke of making her choice of specialisation with that in mind. She is an oncologist, working with people with cancer. She chose not to specialise in working with children as she experienced her high levels of empathy as detrimental to her wellbeing and her objective approach.

Beware the vortex of despair

When we get sucked too much into feeling what others feel, we can become stuck ourselves.

> We can pull each other into the
> 'vortex of despair'.

Compassion is a space where we understand people's feelings. We can be a safety net of support, but we don't go right into the feelings with them.

Empathy silos

I find that cultures with a high level of resistance have 'empathy silos'. People are welded together to protect each other from the other 'mean' people. Empathy is only going so far here – just to the people who are in the same vortex of despair and who think the same way I do. Don't get me wrong – I think empathy is an underdeveloped skill in many workplaces. It is a muscle that would be good to exercise more often whenever we are frustrated with each other. It just needs to extend to people we don't understand or like.

Paul Bloom has just published a book on empathy that is a fascinating read. Called *Against Empathy: the Case for Rational Compassion*, Bloom's book is dedicated to the research and the perspectives that suggest that empathy is dividing us at a social and global level. We become very aligned with people who think in a similar way, and it separates us further from people who believe differently. He believes that empathy is dangerous when used for moral decisions and that we should use reasoning and compassion. His book is a fascinating read.

Courage and kindness

We could all do with people being kinder to each other. I have worked with many leaders over the years who have great compassion for their people and their customers. The two values that they believe drive them the most are courage and kindness. Courage to make the hard decisions. Courage to be able to shift and make the change. But they do it with a real compassion for where people are at – with kindness. Kindness helps them to be thoughtful about treating people well.

Kindness is an act of compassion

Kindness is an action. When we have compassion, we're able to hold someone in a connected space, so they feel we are there supporting them; whereas kindness is an act of compassion. Sometimes firm boundaries are an act of compassion. Someone might be in a state where what they need is for some rules to be put in place so that they're able to cope with what's going on for them. When we develop our ability to be compassionate, we can act in a kind way.

The outcomes of compassion

When we build the compassion so essential to trust, our team becomes a connected whole – a tribe. It is not only from the leader to the tribe; it's between the tribe members as well. When a leader brings compassion to the people they lead, everyone manages change better. People feel supported through change rather than set adrift. They feel understood about what they are going through. Leaders and team members then put in the supports that people need to thrive, rather than drown.

If there is no real understanding of each other's feelings and the impact change is having, we can't even dream of having a functioning team.

> How can we see the world from our clients' perspective, if we can't even do it with the person sitting next to us?

Teamwork in the 'I-centred' society

In the last 15 years, the world has hurtled into more materialism and commercialisation than ever before. We've become an 'I-centered society'. Judith E. Glaser, a world leader in building trust in organisations through conversations, coined the word 'I-centric'. We will look more at her seminal work in this space in Chapter Nine. Her work is used around the world moving organisations from 'I-centric' cultures to trusting 'we-centric' cultures. When we centre on 'I', we feel disconnected; we feel isolated. We've talked throughout this book about the lack of engagement that's going on for people in the workplace; compassion is a way to create a step towards each other rather than keeping the disengagement going.

While I was working with a group going through a medical leadership program one person came in quite late. She seemed a little bit harried and out of sorts, but jumped straight in and started working with us. We were at the stage of developing relationships. People in the room didn't know each other at this point. We were creating an environment for deep learning and dialogue so that we could get some profound insights into leadership. These learning environments need high psychological safety within the participants.

Through the day, the latecomer was flighty and spoke quickly and seemed quite nervous. Towards the end of the day, she had settled. When we began an open discourse about support, compassion and being able to manage ourselves in a high-stress job, she disclosed to the group the sense of anxiety that she often feels walking into work because of what she's been dealing with: getting her two children under six settled for the day. She said that very morning her five-year-old sat stiff as a board so she could not put him into the child seat to take him to kindergarten because he was so distressed at her leaving. That was part of her reason for being late.

Glue

Around the room, the other participants expressed compassion for her. Many others in the room were mothers who could totally connect with high empathy. Others were able to see the distress that had caused her. The tragedy is that she could never disclose that in her everyday job; it's just not done in the environment where she works. The stress levels and the anxiety levels remain constant for her because she doesn't have the support to be able to share what's going on, and just feel a bit at ease and that it is ok.

Just the opportunity to share it with people that she felt safe with quieted her anxiety. It was only a few hours after the event, but we had built, strong rapport within the group and strong compassion for each other, to be able to say, 'What we're trying to do in this course is develop how we lead but also who we are as human beings'. She wasn't asking for us to do anything. It was simply an opportunity to talk about the fact that where we're at emotionally impacts on how well we can work. The fact that she had such a heightened state, and high cortisol, the fear chemical running in her brain, meant that it had to settle before she was able to get into her learning. In the workplace, with that compassion missing, she has to put much more energy into getting into the right state of mind to focus.

Build compassion between your team members

Sometimes the simplest actions can make a big difference to the feeling of compassion between team members. That's great news, isn't it?

> You don't need a big training budget;
> you don't need to change anyone.

Every single member of your team and every leader is already an expert in these behaviours. All they need to do is start using them in the workplace, as much as they use them at home, and with friends and family.

1. 'See' people.
2. Value contributions authentically.
3. Be aware of your impact and your connection, and be kind.

Let's look in more detail at each of these steps.

'See' people

Ubuntu is a southern African term that says 'I am what I am because of who we all are'. It's a philosophy that identifies the connection of a person to others, and that we are nothing if not connected to others. It puts the tribe above the individual. This beautiful African philosophy is an excellent guide to the whole sense of tribe. It says we are not anything if we are not something together. The connection and kindness that ubuntu pulls from this is the basis of the compassion element of trust.

Another beautiful saying that comes from the same area is the greeting that is given, of *sawabona*, which means, 'I see you'. The response, *ngikhona*, means 'I am here'. These evocative greetings pay homage to the deep connection when people are valued for their contribution and for who they are as individuals.

In my filing cabinet at home, I have a letter that was given to me by one of my first principals. At the end of the year, she wrote a letter to every single one of her staff. The letter was not just a generic thank you for the year's work, but it outlined the strengths of what I had brought to the school and specifically identified what I added to the team, the whole school, and to the students.

When I look back at it now, quite a few decades later, I know that I probably was a teacher that thought she knew it all when I first started. I am sure I drove the teachers with more experience up the wall with my overenthusiasm. I'm sure there are ways that I behaved that drove people to distraction. My leader chose to see the positive things that I brought to the school, and highlight them. That letter is something that I hold dear many, many years later.

Seeing people for who they are, and taking notice of what they distinctly bring to our team, is a mindful activity that raises our compassion for others. When I work with teams to develop their tribe, I will often get them to finish their time together sharing one-on-one what they feel the other person brings to the team. The oxytocin levels of joy in the room are raging when we finish this honouring of each other. Those who are focused on becoming real 21st-Century Tribes make conversations like that a ritual.

Seeing without the labels

If you were to sit down and write down the words that others would describe you with, what would they be?

We can have labels in our heads that are not useful for people. Labels such as arrogant, bossy, lazy, stubborn. Whenever we have labels like these, we darken the lens that we see them through. We look through a lens of 'they're not good enough', a lens of 'they're a problem', rather than focusing on the qualities that they bring.
Think of someone you tend to look at with a bit of a dark

shadow when you describe them. Maybe they're a thorn in your side. Someone that you find it difficult to work with. Write down all the labels that you use in your head. Then think about how they might see themselves. Every name that you can think of has a light side to it. For a person marked as stubborn. How would they label themselves? They probably wouldn't put the word stubborn. They might use the word passionate, strong opinions, firm. Someone you might label as lazy might see themselves as cruisy, spontaneous or going with the flow.

> When we're too attached to these names, we can have what's called a confirmation bias, where we only seek data and input that supports our belief.

Every time we happen to see the person who we code as lazy aimlessly (we assume) chatting with someone else again we get the little tick that says, 'Yep, here they are doing not much'. Every time we see the person we code as stubborn pushing their point, tick, our confirmation bias that they're stubborn gets hit. Our reactions become more about the behaviour than about the context and the conversation. Being able to recode those responses and see the world from the way they see themselves is a significant step towards compassion. Ask yourself, 'How can I understand them and the way they see the world to get a better outcome?'

Glue

Rusty or unpolished?

Evan was a senior manager promoted from within a team I worked with years ago. He learned about confirmation bias. Evan knew that we have a loop where we just scan for information that supports what we believe. Through our work, he had nominated Elizabeth as someone he wanted and needed to build a stronger relationship with. He had thought that Elizabeth was a bit past her prime in terms of her ability to stay up with the job. He also noticed that she rarely spoke to him, especially after his promotion. She wouldn't maintain any eye contact with him and wouldn't talk directly to him. Walking past her one day when she was doing a particularly critical team job, he stopped by her and watched her work. 'You are such a gun at doing that. Where would we be without you doing that for us as a team? Thank you,' then kept on walking. He soon noticed that she started interacting with him again. She began talking with him, and she started becoming a happier, engaged member of the team once more. Such a simple thing. She had just been a bit rusty. No one had paid her work and contribution any attention for a long time. He simply polished her up, metaphorically, and she engaged again.

Some people have been sitting in a team and not being 'seen' for a long time. When you reflect on your team, who might that be?

Seven little things that build trust

I hope you look at this list and say, 'Of course, Tracey we do this in our teams'. I'd love to say that I see these things go on, but for many people in the workplace these distinct ways of seeing people are missing. How can you increase them, and as a team create an environment where people connect through this compassionate element of 'seeing' them?

1. Use people's names
You'll be amazed at how acknowledging someone and using their name builds trust. People feel seen.

2. Acknowledge each other when you arrive at work, and when you enter a room.
One of my clients worked hard at getting her team to do this as a start to her change plan. She knew that if people were not welcoming of each other, they could not do the hard, collaborative work they needed to do. It creates the start of an 'I see you' culture. Even if you've worked with your team for years, greeting each other is a form of honouring the presence of the other person.

3. Admit to others when you've made a mistake.
Admitting to others when you've made a mistake is a significant deposit in the emotional bank account – a willingness to be vulnerable in front of others builds trust. And as we know from our reflections on learning in Chapter Six, celebrating mistakes and failure needs to be part of our culture.

4. Welcome newcomers with open arms.
Get to know them. Be interested in their story. Smile at them. Build trust and get people to high performance quickly by making them feel psychologically safe pronto. When we have not had safe social interactions with others, we code them as foe first. Even a smile can make people feel like you are a friend.

5. Be specific
Talk with people about their particular contribution to the project, the team, the day. Show your appreciation.

Glue

6. Sit and eat lunch with each other. Share joyful stories of lives that are beyond work.
An open time to chat, and chew the fat helps people understand each other in ways formal interactions never do. Food is a fabulous equaliser and is the glue of many tribes.

7. Have tribal rituals of celebration.
Personal milestones such as birthdays, sure, but how about for someone completing a degree or getting their sales target? Or untangling a tricky problem? A shift happening with a difficult client? The team achieving something that surprised them? We thank each other broadly for a job well done as a matter of course, but the intimate moments where we see what the unique qualities that a person has that are different from ours bring us together and deepens our bond.

Value contributions authentically

My great uncle Billy was a prisoner in Changi in Malaysia during the Second World War. As the Japanese retreated, he was moved to Japan to work on the wharves. He had to unload the ships and take off huge bales of rice.

There was an old Japanese couple that lived in a little shack at the end of the wharf. With food very scarce, they were starving. When unloading the rice sacks, Uncle Billy would fill the cuffs of his trousers with a couple of handfuls of rice, as much as he could fit in. Then at the end of his shift, he would give this rice to them.

He helped them to survive the war. Just before he was repatriated, this poor couple who had nothing, wanted to convey how much they valued all he had done for them. They gave him a Japanese tea ceremony. What a beautiful and eloquent way to show how much they appreciated what he had done for them.

One of the ways that I try to show how much I appreciate my clients when I work with a group of people is to remember all their names. For me, it says: 'I want to value you so we can learn deeply together'. My knowing and using people's name is a way that I can show that. I hope that people feel supported, that I care and have compassion for them. People often comment to me how powerful that is. Recognition means much more than money to people. The most meaningful recognition that people want in the workplace has no dollar value.

Paul Zak's research, mentioned at the start of the discussion on trust, shows that oxytocin is the chemical of bonding behaviour. Oxytocin comes about when we feel joy and when we feel connected. It is also present when we feel valued, and we get a sense of reward. How do you value others? What is your way of showing that you value others?

Create a team value project. Get people to share, 'What makes me feel appreciated? Is it people spending time with me? Is it gifts? Is it praise? Is it positive feedback? Is it people taking the time to get to know me?'

> At a workshop of 50 people where I asked this question, every table discussion identified that they wanted more feedback about what they were doing well.

Actioning values is trust at work.

Clue

Say thank you more often

I recently visited an organisation that had in the lunch room a beautiful couch with gorgeous coloured cushions. It was inviting and warm. Along the wall behind it was a gratitude graffiti wall. People would write a small paragraph or sentence about what they were grateful for or who they were grateful to. It changed all the time, as old comments got written over with new ones. Pictures would accompany many of the comments to keep the lighthearted nature of the wall. It became a ritual for that team express their gratitude. Not only speaking it but also having it written was a very powerful expression of what that tribe thought was important.

Stephen Covey, thought leader and author of *The Speed of Trust* and *7 Habits of Highly Effective People*, has created many concepts that have changed people's lives. One of his most powerful is the idea of the emotional bank account. It's an evocative way to represent the intangibles of value. When we build trust, we put emotional money into people's emotional bank account. But we can also withdraw it; relationships with high distrust are well into deficit. I believe that when we don't spend time seeing and valuing people and their contribution, we withdraw a huge amount of emotional coins from our team bank account. People feel undervalued. They feel overlooked, then, disengage and become demotivated.

Admit to being wrong

During my career, I worked as a senior leader in business. We would come in on a Monday morning, and the inbox would be full of what we called SCUD missiles (because they were in the press at the time, due to the Iraq war). SCUD missiles are long-range bombs that cause devastation wherever they explode. If we had an issue, the head of the organisation would sit at home on his computer, fire off semi-abusive emails to people about all the things they've done wrong. People would find them exploding in their inbox on a Monday morning. This type of approach was severely destroying any glue of trust that we had for him. My decision to leave a business that I loved was due to the behaviour of that leader. It was sealed one day in a management meeting listening to him blatantly lie about something that had gone wrong. Two of us around the circle knew without a doubt that he had been entirely responsible. I sat there hearing him rant about the reason why the problem had happened, pointing the finger at everyone else. It made me rage inside. His inauthenticity and dishonesty astonished me. His lack of value of the people around him meant that whatever little emotional bank account he held went into deficit. I was out of there!

One of the ways that you can build trust by valuing people is when they've been right, and you've been wrong. Admitting mistakes is a very reliable builder of credibility. We can have this misguided belief that if we do will be seen as incompetent.

> When people admit to being wrong,
> their credibility rises in people's eyes.

It also firmly places us as a learner – which as we have discussed is a foundational pillar of a 21st-Century tribe.

Victor Perton is a former parliamentarian and former Victorian Commissioner to the Americas. An incredibly generous and interested man, he is the epitome of connection and compassion. He is passionate about Australia and our relationships at the global level. He is often called upon to facilitate high-level negotiations. Relationships are core to his work. In his quest to support Australian

Glue

leaders succeed, he has founded the Australian Leadership Blog, and interviews leaders from a range of companies and organisations. He asks them what the attributes of Australian leaders are and what is important to people they lead. It is a treasure trove of insightful real-life reflections of some of our best leaders. Here are a few examples of excerpts pertinent to the discussion of trust through honesty:

Michael Burge, OAM is the Director of The Australian College of Trauma Treatment:
'Australians want trustworthiness and honesty. These characteristics show who our leaders really are, not who they pretend to be as defined by the most recent poll or spin. When perceived as honest, Australian leaders gain in credibility even when mistakes are made, so long as there is an openness to advice and constructive criticism, from their leadership team and constituents. Honesty builds credibility and trust, which are the foundation to invoke confidence and respect from allies, teammates and constituents.'

Turlogh Guerin Chair, Board of Advisors Council Climate Alliance:
'Followers expect that their leaders will apologise when they are wrong. And they must do it quickly and be sure to do it in earnest. Failing to do this one thing will lose them trust faster than anything else.'

RACV's Julie Green pragmatically calls out those who hide mistakes in the political arena:
'Above all, Australians seek trust and honesty from their leaders. We have seen a lack of this from our political leaders. Generally, Australians have a good 'bullshit' barometer.

I encourage you to subscribe to Victor's blog – it is an excellent way to access the thinking of great leaders. (Australianleadershipblogspot.com.au)

Be aware of your impact and your empathy for others; be kind

The first skill of emotional intelligence is emotional self-awareness, and being able to see our impact from the balcony down onto the dance floor is critical in building compassion. If we don't understand how we affect others, it's going to be very hard for us even to be able to see the world from their perspective. My boss just described had little idea of his impact on his team. His self-awareness centred totally on himself and how others affected him. His approach was one of bullying, and it created a toxic environment of distrust. There was no kindness in evidence.

Kindness isn't hard. It's the little things that are the big things. Acts of kindness are beautiful for the world; they make us feel good. If we all did more kind things during our day imagine how we can impact how valued people feel. Here are some small acts of kindness to try:

When you're making your cup of tea, make one for someone else.

Next time you're in busy traffic on your way to work, usher someone into the lane in front of you.

Smile at someone when they come into the room.

Include someone in conversation who might otherwise be a bystander.

Offer to take on a job so that a parent can get to the school concert on time.

Remember what a colleague was doing on the weekend, and ask them about it on Monday.

Glue

Chapter Summary

Having purpose motivates us to be better.

When we connect to purpose and to each other, extraordinary things are possible. Be nice; you'll be happier. Compassion creates connection. The world could do with more compassion. Show small acts of kindness every day.

In *An Everyone Culture: Becoming a deliberately developmental organisation,* 2016, by Robert Kegan and Lisa Laskow Lahey, the authors believe we have two roles. One is our job, and the other is covering up our weaknesses. Covering what it is we are feeling, and what we are thinking. We posture and show ourselves to our best advantage – protecting the 'I'. The amount of energy that goes into having this veneer is enormous in regard to the impact on a team and the cost to the organisation.

Wouldn't it be great if we were part of a place where it just felt nice to be there? Where people felt understood by each other? If we didn't have to hide away our fears and our aspirations? Imagine if we connected through compassion and kindness. Linked by seeing the potential, the diversity and the good things we bring to the team, rather than what we'd like to change or remove.

What's next?

We're at the pointy end of trust. We're at the pointy end of the whole book. All the chapters of the book are leading towards this last element, this last skill. If we don't get better at doing this skill, we will never achieve any of the collaboration, any of the glue of trust, build any of the bonds that we are seeking.

This skill is the outward manifestation of the compassion, connection and collaborative elements of our glue.

It's the art of conversation.

9 Conversation

> **To get from good to great depends on the culture, which depends on the relationships, which depends on the conversation.**
>
> Judith E. Glaser, *Conversational Intelligence: How great leaders build trust and get extraordinary results*

If connection and compassion are the adhesive and cohesive of trust, then conversation is the tool that mixes them together. Collaborative conversation is the outward manifestation of trust. Quality conversations of teams and individuals working together elevate the trust level so that you can do extraordinary work. It helps to clarify assumptions, explore new ideas, become more creative and innovative, and create a commitment to action.

We know that everyone talks, everyone learns to speak from a very early age and it's an important part of being in the work environment. The quality is poor on average, talking at each other rather than talking with each other. Without the right type of conversations, assumptions run rampant. In the absence of any information, and distrust in place, people fill in the missing parts with the worst scenario. When we have a lack of conversation in the workplace, we fill that void with the chatter and worries that are in our head. Unless there is a substantial body of trust we quickly fall into a space where we assume the worst and feel dislocated.

Without high-quality conversations, the fear chemical cortisol raises in our head. Silos stay in place and distrust festers. Trust becomes further and further away. Connection and compassion focused on learning, growth and collaboration are the drivers for quality conversations. We strengthen our ability to understand each other, to understand the work, and to challenge each other to move forward.

When we have a conversation with no *connection*, we stay isolated from one another, and our collective purpose is missing. When we don't have collaborative conversations, we can't get to a space of learning out loud and testing out our thinking. We can't piggyback on other people's ideas. Our ability to create and innovate together just isn't there. The conversations are either stilted, guarded or not in existence. Or there's simply someone telling you what to do.

When we have a conversation with no *compassion*, it lacks the empathy that we need to have for each other and our clients. We are unable to see the world from their perspective. It keeps us stuck in our own thinking. We are unable to move to a 'we thinking' and collective 'our-thinking' place.

This is the keystone of the book. None of the outcomes already outlined will occur if we don't have connected, compassionate conversations that count. Without collaborative conversations that challenge the status quo, we're going nowhere, and we end up becoming stagnant and atrophying, as an organisation, into oblivion.

Tracey Ezard

Dismantling the 'Berlin Wall'

In my second year of teaching, I worked at a primary school. It was right next to a secondary school, and we shared a big staffroom. It was all brand spanking new and everyone went in there with high expectations of commitment and collaboration. With the secondary college, it would mean that we could increase the quality of the education we were giving to our students. The staffroom had been open for a couple of years when I got there. I discovered that all the primary staff sat in one part of the staffroom and all the secondary staff took up the three-quarters of the staffroom, and no one spoke in depth to each other. Even when we came in to get cups of coffee, and the secondary teachers were standing and making coffee, there was no real dialogue beyond formalities. It was like there was an insurmountable wall up between us. It was such a waste.

There were people in both schools doing great stuff that could help our students. They also had incredible facilities, such as drama and technology studios that I was dying to get my kids into. But we were on the wrong side of the 'Berlin Wall'. There was no interaction. A colleague of mine decided that this situation was ridiculous. Whenever she had time off during classes to do preparation and marking, she would take all her work down into the staffroom and sit there on the big tables. She'd spread her work out, and when she saw people, she would put her head up and say, 'Hello,' and catch their eye.

Then, one day, a secondary English teacher stopped when he passed her and complimented her on the student projects on the table. He was amazed at the quality and how they apparently expected too low a standard in Year 7 if they could achieve that in Year 4! That moment, everything changed because he was willing to start a conversation. All those efforts would have come to nothing if he

Glue

had not reached out. That broke the seal, I suppose, and we all started having more frequent conversations about students, about work, about our different approaches. And that led to co-creating conversations where we looked at working together to increase the education of the students that we taught.

We started to do some cross-tutoring. We exposed each other to the type of thinking that we did in the primary and the type of thinking done in the secondary school. Without that first curious conversation, we would never have shifted the status quo. A trusting relationship started.

In this final chapter, I am going to show you how to have interesting, co-creating conversations, based on connection and compassion, which create the glue of a solid team.

There are three main areas we will look at:

Have co-creating conversations

Co-creating conversations happen when, by being together, we make something more. Co-creation is when we work together to bring something to life that wasn't there before in each of our minds. There is an energy that ignites when we are in co-creation mode. Have you ever seen a chef using a huge wok throwing in sauces, meats, vegetables and noodles? Quickly served up in the bowl, a sublime meal to tuck into appears. Co-creating conversations are like this dish. It's when everyone's ingredients are included just at the right time to achieve an end result. We don't know what the end result is, but it is looked forward to with anticipation. There is a joy and excitement in the process.

Recode conflict

The path to co-creating conversation involves 'recoding' conflict. When we can have our 'work' conversations with energy and passion, we have already mastered the art of conflict. We see debate and challenging of thinking as critical seasoning to our discussion.

When still learning to do this, we can be afraid of a conflict of opinions so we avoid going anywhere near them. Too often, we have elephants that sit in the room, and we're not game to talk about them. We must talk about them. Respectful challenge in conversations should be a way of *increasing* our trust and improving our understanding of each other. If we don't talk about them, we leave the elephants bouncing around us for everyone to feel, but not deal with.

Agile listening

The third and essential element needed to stimulate co-creating conversations is be agile in our listening. In conventional environments, we simply listen only for when other people stop talking so that we can start our turn. Agile listening is for teams who are armed and ready with a strong learning environment to push the flames of creativity.

Glue

Co-creation

Talk with, not *at* or *to* people.

Having quality conversations increases the oxytocin, dopamine and serotonin that leads to trust. It enables us to work with the executive function engaged and builds that trust. When we have conversations that raise cortisol, we withdraw from the executive function, and our ability to have empathy, connect, collaborate, problem solve, decreases rapidly. As we discussed in Chapter Six, this is critical to the collaborative learning environment so needed in organisations today.

Judith E. Glaser is the creator of Conversational Intelligence® and Chairman of the CreatingWe Institute. Her work has transformed many major company cultures, moving them from low trust to high trust. Conversational Intelligence® or C-IQ is the vehicle for this shift. Based on the neuroscience of trust and the *quality* of our conversations, Judith's large body of work and research has given us excellent tools to view our conversations through and build our conversational intelligence.

C-IQ uses a conversational dashboard that takes people through three levels. When we have conversations, our brain is clueing in carefully into whether the person we are talking with is trustworthy. If their behaviours are ones that build trust, our brains function more in our prefrontal cortex (PFC). The PFC is also known as the executive function. It is where we problem solve, collaborate, connect and learn. It is also where empathy for others resides.

If we unconsciously or consciously pick up what our brains deem as 'untrustworthy' behaviours, or we are uncertain, our limbic brain takes over, driven by the amygdala and we can retreat from the PFC. Our actions become more about survival – withdrawal, passive-aggressive behaviour, or attack. Long term conversations like this can end up severely affecting not only relationships but also the ability for people to perform well in the work context.

In general, many of our conversations are trusting and open, producing the chemicals such as oxytocin that help us access the PFC. Cortisol, the fear-inducing chemical, lasts much longer in the body than these chemicals, so we need to understand and minimise/downregulate the behaviours that increase it.

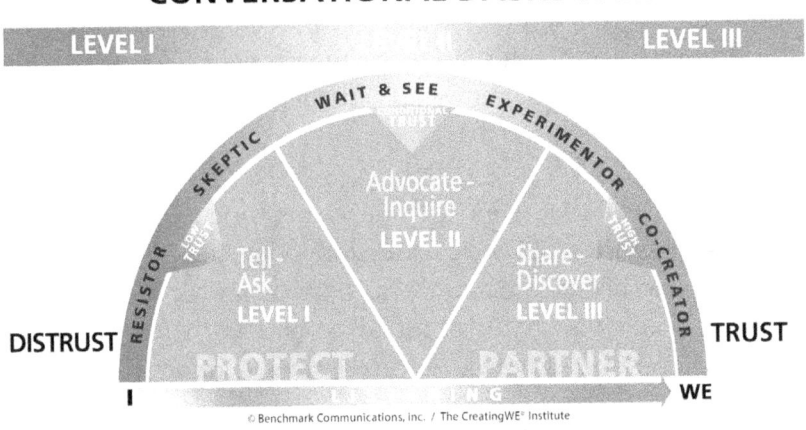

Used with permission Copyright Benchmark Communications, Inc.

Clue

Level 1 conversations on the C-IQ dashboard are the 'ask or tell' level. This level is transactional. It's one person telling another person either what to do or what they think without little interaction. It is the epitome of the 'talking at' approach, a didactic interaction. Information disseminated with no discussion. If you recall an 'average' meeting, you'll recognise Level I straight away! I always imagine an army sergeant yelling orders when I think of the extreme of this level. We can get caught in what Judith E. Glaser calls the 'tell-yell-sell syndrome'. When we ignore perspectives, or don't ask opinions, we create a space where there's no conversation entered, causing us to distrust. When this is the predominant mode of speaking, we fire off cortisol in our brain, and this causes us to withdraw from the prefrontal cortex. The Level 1 conversation of the C-IQ dashboard is the area of distrust and resistance.

Level II C-IQ is the Inquire and Advocate level. 'I have a perspective, and I'm willing to listen to yours, but my main aim is to advocate for my position.' It's where conditional trust sits. We allow each other to voice opinions. The primary goal is to promote our point of view. Trust rises, but we are still sceptical because it is about agenda and positioning.

Many middle leaders I work with have this issue with their senior leaders. They go to see them tease something out. They want to pose an idea and co-create a new way with them. For senior leaders who haven't uncovered the secret to co-creating with their team the default of Level II conversations is their comfort zone. When the idea is put forward with hopes of creating something further together the senior leader simply says, 'Well, what I think you should do is...' It's not a space for creating something more. It's a space of, 'I hear your opinion. This is my opinion. Glad to hear yours, but I'm not interested in actually looking at a third alternative.' Level II is about influencing through personal or positional power.

Level III is the pinnacle of the conversational dashboard, the transformational conversation. Conversational Intelligence® used in organisations to transform culture and therefore business, is about building the capability to have these conversations. This level is the Transformational level of 'share and discover' conversations. It's an open, connected and transparent space where we ask questions for which we have no answers. It helps us not only cooperate but move up the collaborative continuum to co-creation. When we are open to influence and exhibit conversational behaviours that build trust, we increase our oxytocin, dopamine and serotonin.

I would strongly recommend you read Judith E. Glaser's books, starting with *Conversational Intelligence: How great leaders build trust and get extraordinary results*, 2014. I have had the honour of learning first hand from Judith over the last few years. Her insight into human behaviour and the importance of connection and trust are astounding, as is her warmth and generosity in sharing her knowledge. Her work and the work of the CreatingWe Institute is creating a lasting legacy on the world, as business, education and other sectors use it to transform the way they have conversations.

Shifting the need to be right

In Chapter Six – Collaborative Inquiry and Deeper Learning, we discussed the dopamine hit we get when we feel vindicated and right. When this is happening frequently, we could be stuck in Level I conversations. This increases cortisol in others. If you know that your need to be right can sometimes override your brain and the way you hold conversations, here are some suggestions for next time the 'need to be right' rises strongly. A few steps that can teach your brain to step into a space of trust, collaboration and creation:

CLue

PAUSE – Take an inward breath and increase your awareness of what is happening in your brain and body. Consciously awaken your awareness to how your drive to be right might be 'hijacking' the way that you are interacting and thinking.

OPEN – Visualise an image that represents your mind opening to take on new learning.

LISTEN – Focus and be present to the others in the room and their perspectives.

CHALLENGE – Push yourself to challenge your own thinking and judgements – 'What if there is another way to look at this? Am I limiting the possibilities here? What do others think, feel and believe about this?'

ASK – Artful questions allow you and the group to be curious and explore the thinking and perspectives in the room: 'Tell me more; What does look like to you? I'm interested in finding more about what you think there…'

Collaborative environments are not win/lose or win/win. They are a gain for everyone.

Talk about the why and the who, not just the what and the how

I've talked a lot in this book about purpose. I've talked about connecting to each other and the importance of relationships. We often do not make the time to do that. Spending time and getting back to the why is such a critical element of conversation. We go straight to task too readily. We talk about how we're going to do this and don't spend time having conversations, co-creating our purpose for our goals or the project. Spending that time is time well spent. It means we have the connection and the trust in each other that we are all heading in the same direction.

A little exercise:

As a team, think back over your last few meetings and apply this key to the 'discussions' you had. Use my DICE model to work how where you spend most of your meeting time:

D – Decide
A decision needs to be made by the group in the room. Dialogue is required to come to a decision. The depth of this discussion is contextual and can range from simple affirmative nods around the room, or more robust debate.

I – Inform
Information dissemination and sharing. Keeping people in the loop about things going on. One person speaking.

C – Consult
Decisions made in different parts of the organisation or hierarchy are needing input and opinion. These decisions are collected and then considered within a process elsewhere. The cynics might say that this is where those in authority who have already made the decision tick the checkboxes. Consultation carried out well though can be a wonderful way to get ideas, input and insights from a cohort of people along the way to help with co-creation.

E- Explore

The space of co-creation. Discovering our ideas, putting forward insights, data, analysis and exploring the space.

Glue

What proportion of time are you in **I** – inform? **I** is the danger zone for collaboration. Sure, it's important stuff, but if telling people about things takes up most of your time together, people want to bang their heads down onto the table with boredom and frustration. Or they escape into the vortex of their emails. What other processes can be used to cut down the amount people are talked *at?*

How much time do you make for **E** – explore? In this mode, we are employing all the learner roles discussed in Chapter Six. Sensemaker, Challenger, Experimenter and Supporter come out to play as we explore. Now is the time to talk about purpose. It's talking *with* people to co-create the future actions. It is the creative and innovative time to play with possibilities. Increase the time you spend having conversations here, will grow not only with the momentum for change but also trust.

The DICE key can be used to plan meetings, so people are clear what role they will play during the meeting.

Foster curiosity by being curious

When curiosity is a mainstay of a team, we get more familiar with testing out our thinking and sharing that thinking with each other. It helps with collaboration and learning-out-loud approach. People asking, 'Why is it that you think that? What is the reason behind that? What would it look like if we …? How might we…?' When we have a curious mind, we start to move into a wondering perspective that helps us to co-create new ways of working. That space of wondering is such a lovely space to be in for our brain. It kicks off our internal motivation and off our ability to learn. There have been studies that show that when people are curious, it also increases our memory retention, as has been discussed in the Learning chapter.

Think about the times that you've been curious. Reflect on a conversation you recently had. Think about yourself as to how many questions did you ask. It is also important when having meaningful conversations about performance. I often use the Pareto 80/20 Principle. Most performance discussions are made up of a leader speaking 80% of the time and 20% from the person whose performance is the subject. Imagine if we could flip that. What if we took an unusual position and asked the other person what they feel and think first? What is it that they hope to do in the future? What skills do they wish to build? Where are their challenges? Then we need to shut up and just listen and hear what they've got to say.

Before you walk into a meeting, take five minutes to write down all the things you're curious about, about whatever the purpose of the meeting is. In the meeting, find out what other people are curious about regarding the issue at hand and then have those conversations.

> The curious mind is endlessly searching
> for different interpretations of
> the world.

When we become comfortable with curiosity, it becomes a safe place to challenge our thinking. It becomes safe to challenge our assumptions because we don't sit with the status quo of our thoughts. It allows us to question our individual and team thinking in a wondering way rather than in a judging way. Remember my curious friend Andrew from Chapter Six? I love sitting down talking with him. He is fascinating and fascinated. He's fascinated with how people see the world, what people think, how cultures work, how teams work. He asks interesting questions to find out what others think. I love hearing the questions that he asks because they are artful and don't come from a position of judgement at all. They originate from

Glue

a natural wonder and curiosity at the world. If we could all do more of that, then the world would be a more interesting and trusting place because it would be safe to think about different alternatives.

Use visual processes that enable collective discussions

John Medina, the author of *Brain Rules: 12 Principles for surviving and thriving at work, home, and school*, 2004, states that that vision trumps all senses.

> Research on retention shows that the ability for people to remember things they have been told in words beyond three days is 10%. Using images only, it jumps up to 35%, but when we put words and pictures together, it jumps to 65%.

When I work with teams, we always work visually. We create the picture of who we are and where we're heading. What's the picture of our vision? What does it look like if we're able to draw it up? What is the purpose? What are the principles that are driving us? If we were to create that as a shape, what would it look like? If we were to draw a picture of it, what would we see? Identify the challenges and the achievements. Put it all up to see it and for us to have a collective, co-creating conversation about what we need to do next. That enables collective discussion.

What happens if I can't draw?

It doesn't matter. It's not about whether it comes out looking any good. What it is about, is about the process of creating it together.

It's the conversation that we had to have so that we know what it means. I'm yet to find anyone that can't just do a stick figure. The teams that can create visual artefacts that help to guide their journey anchor firmly to it. Sam Kaner, an American facilitation thought leader, says, 'I can't believe that a group of people can come to a decision that is not written out and displayed in a public way'. There are screeds and screeds of words written down that teams do every year about their goals, what they're going to do, how they're going to do it, that never get looked at ever again. Put it up and be proud of it!

Recode conflict

The word 'conflict' raises a lot of internal baggage for us. When I ask people what they think of conflict, they imagine aggression, fighting, confrontation. It is a terminology that pushes us away. We believe when we raise issues that we are worried about or challenged about, others will see it as conflict and therefore unpleasant. If we go back to what's happening in the brain, there is a fear of and anxiety about speaking the truth. So, we shut down from it. Our cortisol levels are up because we're worried about what will happen if we do tell the truth. Some of this comes from our experience of disagreement in our personal lives. The imprint of arguments and unhealthy ways of dealing with conflict when we were growing up gets carried into the workplace.

Talk about the elephants

When we don't talk about our challenges and what we are worried about, they end up becoming huge elephants that almost take up the whole room. As Kegan and Lahey discuss in *An Everyone Culture: Becoming a deliberately developmental organisation*, 2016, an enormous amount of energy is consumed on what is not discussed.

Glue

At the beginning of some journeys with teams, they can seem harmonious and appear to get along. When we begin conversations about purpose they seem connected. But when we talk about what might be stopping them, it becomes apparent that the challenges have been swept under the carpet. Often when there is a fear of conflict, passive-aggressive behaviour comes out instead. Passive-aggressive behaviour is when snide comments occur. Instead of having a conversation with one other person, I'll go and complain about it to someone else and not discuss it the person directly. I don't want to talk about how I feel to the person involved. It pushes behaviour underground. There is a lack of psychological safety to be able to have the conversation.

The Italians have a saying: 'Don't put the fish under the table'. If we don't talk about things that matter and hide them under the table, they start stinking. They fester, and it's a horrible environment to be in. If we mix our animal metaphors, you can see the elephants bouncing around the room, and you can smell the fish that's stinking from under the table.

Be brave

If you know your team is in a place of distrust and no compassion, no conversations and no connections, this feels incredibly risky. My suggestion to you is to get a facilitator in to help you raise team issues in a safe environment.

Get someone skilled at getting the conversation started and creating a safe environment for people. The team will need to be able to say what is going on for them and what's worrying them about their work. To do that we need to create an environment that lowers cortisol – the fear-inducing chemical – and increases oxytocin.

Unless we regulate fear down, it won't work. We need to spend time creating the connection. A place that allows people to talk to each other with curiosity, understand who we are, and increase all the elements discussed in the Connection chapter. We want to find out what people's skills are. Celebrate their achievements. Celebrate their successes. Lower the cortisol by increasing the connection and compassion.

Build your team's RID muscle

Trust and reward increases when people feel connected to each other. It helps us take the first step towards having safe, great debate. Rather than conflict, I call it Robust Ideological Debate (RID). Instead of fighting or posturing, it's discussing the things that matter to us as a team. It takes away the personal and gets to the real conversation. How can we thrive and what is the work that we need to do? Psychological safety is the thing that gets teams to high-performing tribes – they feel safe to talk about the elephants.

One of the best leaders that I have ever seen in action, Sarah, is a brilliant RID facilitator. Sarah is also a transformational leader who creates individual connection and trust with her people. Walk around her organisation and you can see that they co-create a safe environment for people to be who they are. They celebrate each other and show gratitude. Their purpose and principles are evident in everything they do. They have elephants on the meeting agenda. It's a fun way to remind them as a tribe to raise issues before they become elephants. They make sure that as a team, and as an organisation, the culture is one of, 'Let's talk about stuff that's not working or worrying us before it gets too hard, too big and too hurtful'.

Encourage people to step into that space as early as you can. Be honest about what you are all trying to do. It's not about the leader

Glue

going in and pointing fingers. It's about the leader co-creating an environment with everyone to say, 'If we are going to succeed, we need to be able to do it in a way that helps everyone'. When there are challenges, we see them as opportunities to grow, not opportunities to shut down.

What are the hot topics?

Just as you can build your curiosity muscle, you can build your RID muscle as a team. Start by co-creating a list of hot topics that challenge you as a team. Write them all down. Have a brainstorm session where you write them separately first. What change would you like to see? Where is it that things are not working? Have everyone make a list and then put them together as a team. Work out which ones are critical. You will see a theme come through.

I did this with a group of 70 individuals in a workshop recently. From all around the tables, there was a strong theme of three major issues that were affecting everyone in that room. If that organisation doesn't sit down and have some real conversations about, 'How can we co-create a solution to this?' then they are missing a tremendous opportunity to move to high performance.

Start with the easy ones first

To build your team RID muscle, get the list of hot topics and test them out. Pick a low priority one, and experiment with some processes to tease out the thinking. Use a facilitator to start with if that helps, or someone from another team with that skill if you don't feel confident enough to do it yourselves. Think about your collaborative mindset. How can you have great ideological debate without going to the personal? Use it as an experiment. Have someone from another team or a mentor come in, watch and give their observations afterwards. Have the team debrief how it went. It is such a critical team skill, and we don't spend time building its capability.

> When the Robust Ideological Debate muscle develops and flexes, the team is so much stronger.

Then add a bit of chilli

As the muscle gets stronger, move to the hard ones. Make sure you start with the principles that allowed you to work well with the lower priority ones. What are the norms that worked for everyone? When a marathon runner starts training, they don't go straight for the marathon. They build up their running strength. They build up their endurance. Do the same thing with having these conversations, those that can often go to conflict. Recode them into a robust ideological debate and as you do it, have a bit of fun with it. Try some different things. Use post-it notes. Create large charts that clearly identify the issues that challenge you. Be curious about it and develop that wonder about these hot topics rather than fear.

The tone of your voice changes the meaning of what you say

The *way* we have any team or individual conversation can build or destroy trust. The tonality in which we deliver our words is an underestimated treasure. We are aiming for an authentic, curious tone when we're in the space co-creating together. The tonality that we're after is invitational yet challenging. When we speak in an invitational way, we are in an 'I wonder' position. Dropping the invitation can move it quickly into sounding judgmental. 'Should',

Glue

'must', 'have to', are all words that bring up the defense against attack. They shut down opportunity. If you think of the phrase, 'I'd like to pose another perspective on that decision' and say that in an invitational way, it shows that you're open to influence.

You can also say, 'I don't agree with that,' with a very high, judgmental tone to your voice. Try that now as you're reading. Say, 'I don't agree with that,' in an invitational way and, 'I don't agree with that,' in a judging way. With the invitational lens, there needs be a comment for further conversation. 'I don't agree with that, and I'd like to explore it further …' When it comes from a judging place, we put down our opinion and close off any conversation for further debate. Many teams live in this space of shut down, where there is no opportunity for further discussion. Test out your invitational tonality. Talk about it as a team. How do we create an invitational culture that helps us to step into a place not only of trust but also of learning? That is also helping your RID muscle strengthen.

Write down your questions and see if they're invitational or judging. Have a play around with just saying, 'What were you thinking?' in different ways. Try it in a smooth, tonality, then in a melodious, invitational way. Put the emphasis on different words.

>'*What* were you thinking?'
>
>'What were you *thinking*?'
>
>'What *were* you thinking?'

They are all going to get different responses from people. Now say it with an invitation and genuine curiosity. Being intentional about tonality as a team will build a co-creating environment and build trust.

Agile listening

If we've been talking since we were a baby, we've been listening for even longer, yet listening is one of the most under-developed skills that we have as communicators.

When we sit down and mindfully listen to others and connect to what they're saying, we build a bridge between us that is often missing. It is a big part of the oxytocin levels rising and trust increasing. When we listen to others, we are often formulating what our response is going to be. Recalling conversations, we're often not remembering the conversation, more likely what we were thinking at the time of our conversation. Deep, mindful listening is an art in itself. My good friend and colleague Oscar Trimboli is a thought leader in the art of listening. His book *Deep Listening: Impact beyond words*, 2017 helps us to understand the nuances of this type of listening. One that is slow and mindful and deeply connecting. I love one of his evocative statements – and am probably drawn to it as it is a skill that I constantly need to work on! 'The first ingredient for deep listening is to treat silence like another word in the conversation.'

Stoke the fire

But when the collective energy is high and ideas are ready to explode, we need another trick to our skillset – quick, follow-the-energy type of listening. Listening that helps catch the momentum we are creating and leaps aboard.

Conventional teams are besieged with default behaviour and thinking that is like a bucket of water on co-creation. Some will start saying something, formulating their thinking as they speak. One of the Enlighteners will come in and grab it and then make it

Glue

their own. Someone with a fixed mindset will shut down the creative process with a cynical remark or eye roll. Going around the table to see what everyone thinks makes the work stilted and disjointed. When a team runs on conventional team thinking, this is a painful process. Brilliant thinking stays within the minds of those on the team who will never open their mouths in a meeting. The amount of great thinking that doesn't ever get spoken and so never listened to in a conventional team is a crying shame.

Add the fuel

Let's imagine ourselves in a strong, connected tribe, come together to move a project forward. There is high trust in the group, and they know that now the fun begins! It is time to collaboratively fuel the ideas that have been flickering in people's minds like candle flames. When we are in a co-creation environment, and innovating for future possibilities, there is an excitement and energy present. There is an agility to the quality of the listening. We can drop into deep listening to focus on critical elements of their thinking, and then pop up to grow, extend, ideate and create. Like building a crackling fire, the listening flow is dependent on the quality of the materials burning. A great idea could be sitting in the embers of the fire. In sync as a team, we move down into deep listening to let someone explore their thinking out loud and add oxygen to the ember. We ask wondering questions to help them tease it out. We might sit in silence as we let the idea grow in our minds. Then we start building the fire. Listening to each other, we get drawn to where the fire is hottest. We prepare for it to be chaotic – people are fired up, excited, probably talking over the top of each other and tumbling head long into the spirit of creative chaos.

As we listen, our thinking crackles with ideas. We don't stop them; we enter the flames and throw our log in when the time is right.

Someone jumps up to draw a picture or diagram or writes a word down on a piece of paper to come back to it. There is a large paper in the centre of the table and whiteboards on the wall for people to doodle. Coloured markers and post-it notes are scattered around. This allows the creative process to flow, as people create the visual picture of their discussion. Something is said, and someone else builds upon it, adding their thoughts, insights and skills into the mix. An image appears out of the chaos. The tribe understands what it needs to do next to move things forward. The energy of the fire becomes fierce as we work on ideas that hold fuel for us. It is a co-creation space where no one holds ownership – it is a space of *we*.

The listening in this space is fast moving – we need to be ok with missing things. If we don't feel heard, we need to be willing to bang the table and say 'Oi!' hang on – I think I'm on to something here – bear with me and help me get it out of my head'. It gives brilliant ideas a chance to catch alight. With high trust, this is how a 21st-Century Tribe can roll.

Chapter Summary

Conversations activate the glue of trust.

Have more co-creating conversations. Build the robust ideological debate muscle as a team. Become agile in your listening. Have fun! In my 20 years of experience with this framework, I have seen people and teams transform from bitter conflict and excruciating failure into flourishing, exciting and dynamic tribes. The kind of high performing agile innovators that rise to the top of every market. They have done it by having deep compassionate conversations that build trust and connection.

Conclusion

That's it. You now have a powerful framework that will transform your teams into 21st-Century Tribes.

Let's push the envelope on teams. It's an exciting time to move beyond conventional teams to 21st-Century Tribes. The time is ripe for us to redefine our work environment. Let's create engaged, thriving cultures. Let's make work the place where people feel connected. A place where deep learning is at the basis of the way we collaborate and purpose drives us forward together.

Wherever you might be on the journey from siloed team to 21st-Century Tribe, working on the glue of collaboration and trust will build strong bonds for you to move forward. The future is brighter when our teams are willing to step into a collaborative learning space and solve problems together. When we set our sights on a collective vision and purpose we willingly challenge the status quo. When we treat each other with compassion we are willing to go the extra mile as a team. When we trust each other – anything is possible.

> The little things become the big things.

with thanks

Justin, my husband and rock. His steadfast support and encouragement has made this book a reality. His wonderful partnership and parenting in our family has allowed me to do the work I do with energy and passion, rather than exhaustion. A wonderful man and beautiful human being. Always there – cracking dad jokes, cooking incredible meals. He inspires me to be a better person.

Conor and Layla, my two teenagers. Watching them grow into strong, intelligent and caring people is a joy. They challenge my thinking and encourage me. Always.

My parents, Robyn and Keith Jessup, who have always been our family's biggest support. I am so grateful for their love and care of us all.

My thanks to Judith E. Glaser, who has mentored me in the development of my own Conversational Intelligence. She has been incredibly generous with her time and insights. It has been a joy to work with and learn from her. Thank you to Yvonne Coburn who introduced me to Judith and the CreatingWe world. I am excited about the difference this work will make in the world.

Thank you to Ben Cooper of Chin Chin, Philip Leslie of Glaxo Smith Kline, who gave their time to share their stories with me.

Huge thank you to Victor Perton, founder of the Australian Leadership Blog. His wisdom and insight into leadership, trust and professional relationships has been invaluable.

Pam, who shared her David and Goliath story of battling the bank following the death of her son. Your courage in the face of adversity inspires me, as does your unfailing compassion for humans in general.

Thank you to Kath Walters for her guidance through the writing of this book. Her process, support and insight has been invaluable.

Suzie Leyden, my Business Manager, has changed my life! Her commitment to our business and care of what we are creating has huge impact on me and our clients.

To my gang – the friends who support me and make me laugh. I am blessed with a wonderful bunch of girls who keep me sane: Karin White, Ree Pritchard, Gina Ezard, Donna McGeorge, Maree Burgess, Kim Ryan, Deb Dalziel, Kate Gosnell, Kirsty Grace and Jac Pontefract. The men in their lives are pretty special too!

This book was shaped in the presence of genius – so thank you to those who added their thoughts and insights along the way. Matt Church your uncanny, laser thinking has elevated my thinking on tribes. Kieran Flanagan – your playful riff on Glue was a catalyst for the way I approached the book. Jane Anderson, thank you for your enthusiasm and approach to my professional triber work and unwavering support. Lynne Cazaly, Donna McGeorge and Maree Burgess – my accountability buddies, idea bouncers and general cheer crew – gratitude and joy from the bottom of my glue jar!

And finally, to Matt Church and Peter Cook and all my friends in the Australian Thought Leader community. Without you, this book would be nothing but a little thought in my head.

About Tracey Ezard

In a fast-moving world, teams need to form, storm and norm fast to connect and collaborate for extraordinary outcomes. Galvanising teams quickly and creating a BUZZ is Tracey's forte.

Tracey has worked with over 20,000 people globally through facilitation and culture building in teams going through mergers, restructures or intact teams reconnecting to purpose, culture, strategy and values.

She is a Professional Triber.

Like a Hollywood director, Tracey understands the challenges of bringing teams together to move collectively with impact. Leaders use Tracey to set the frameworks for collaboration and to create cultures where people come together to achieve amazing things.

She transforms Teams to become Tribes and Leaders to become Tribers. This momentum future-proofs organisations, retains talent, explodes engagement, reduces complacency and the status quo.

An in-demand keynote speaker, she inspires and challenges her audiences to think differently about how they connect and commit at a deeper level. Conference organisers have described her as invitational yet challenging.

Tracey is also the author of *The Buzz, Creating a Thriving & Collaborative Learning Culture.* She is Fellow of the Australian Council for Educational Leaders (Vic Branch)

Visit Tracey's website or email her at
tracey@traceyezard.com

www.traceyezard.com

www.ingramcontent.com/pod-product-compliance
Lightning Source LLC
Chambersburg PA
CBHW050308010526
44107CB00055B/2159